MY FIRST
Christmas Piano Music

Easy-to-Play Holiday Songs for Kids

Emily Norris

Illustrated by Malgorzata Detner

Z Kids • New York

CONTENTS

Introduction

Hi, friends!

My name is G-sharp the Giraffe. If you were on our earlier journeys together in *My First Piano Lessons* and *My First Piano Sheet Music*, you will recognize me. If this is your first time meeting me, welcome! I'm so excited to meet you.

This book has my favorite Christmas music to play on piano. I've shortened some of the songs to make them easier to play for beginners, just like you! Even if you are a brand-new piano player, you will find these songs easy to learn and fun to play.

Many of these songs will be familiar to you and will get you into the Christmas spirit! You might even convince your family to sing along while you play. Some of the songs might be new to you, but I hope you will find them just as fun to learn and sing along to.

The first songs are easier, and the last songs are a little harder, but all the songs in the book are simple. You can play the songs in order or flip through to any song you want to play—it's your choice! And don't worry! For the songs that are a little harder, I will leave a note or two on the page to help you through the tricky parts.

Just like on our other journeys together, remember:

Journeys can be tiring.
So take breaks!

Journeys can be hard.
It's OK to make mistakes!

Journeys are exciting.
So let's have fun!

Jolly Old Saint Nicholas

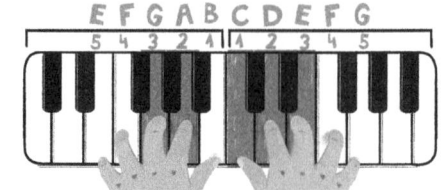

Jol - ly   old Saint   Nich - o - las,   lean your ear this   way.

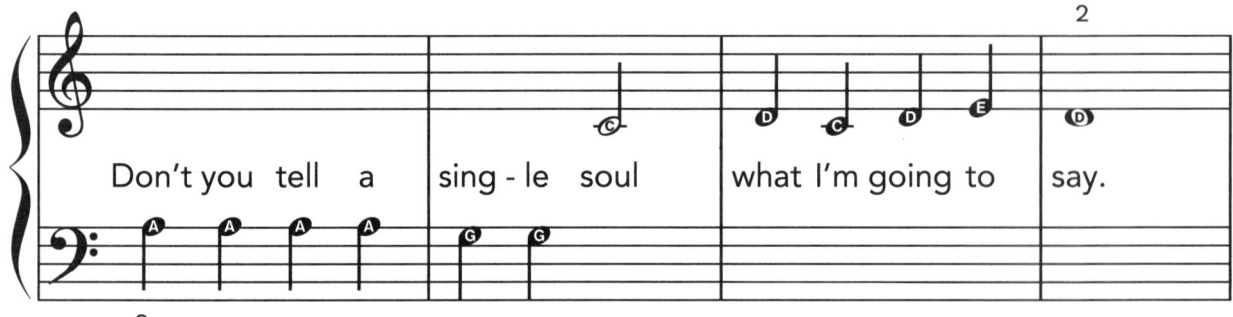

Don't you tell   a   sing - le soul   what I'm going to   say.

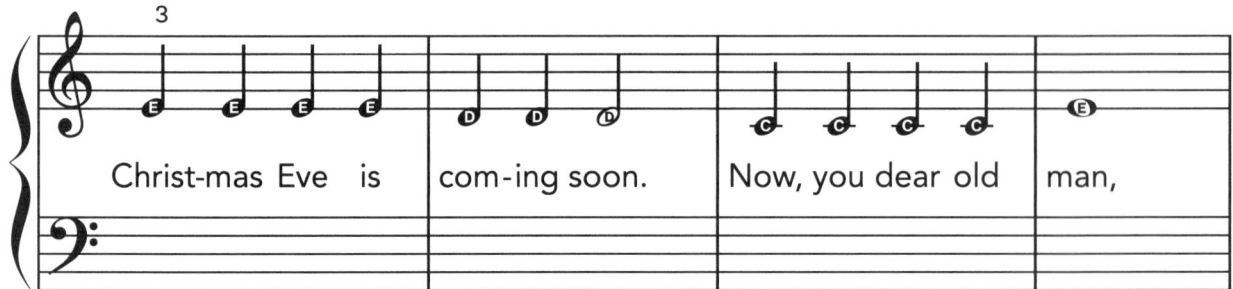

Christ-mas Eve   is   com-ing soon.   Now, you dear old   man,

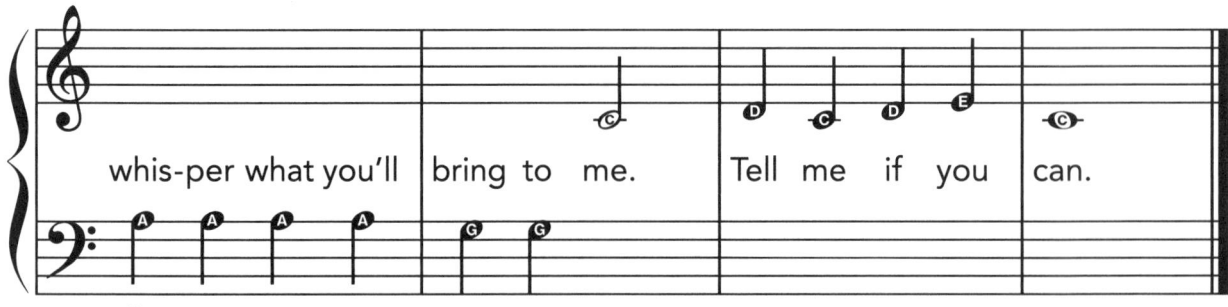

whis-per what you'll   bring to   me.   Tell me   if   you   can.

I Saw Three Ships

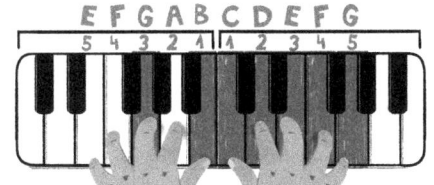

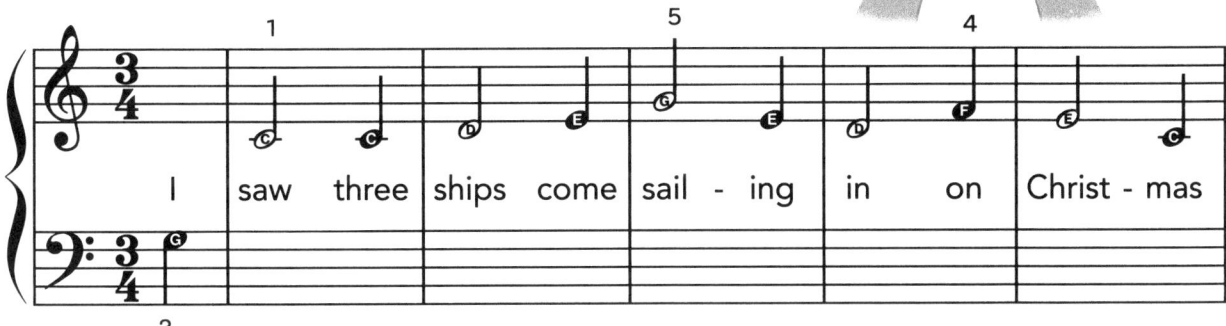

I saw three ships come sail - ing in on Christ - mas

Day, on Christ - mas Day. I saw three ships come

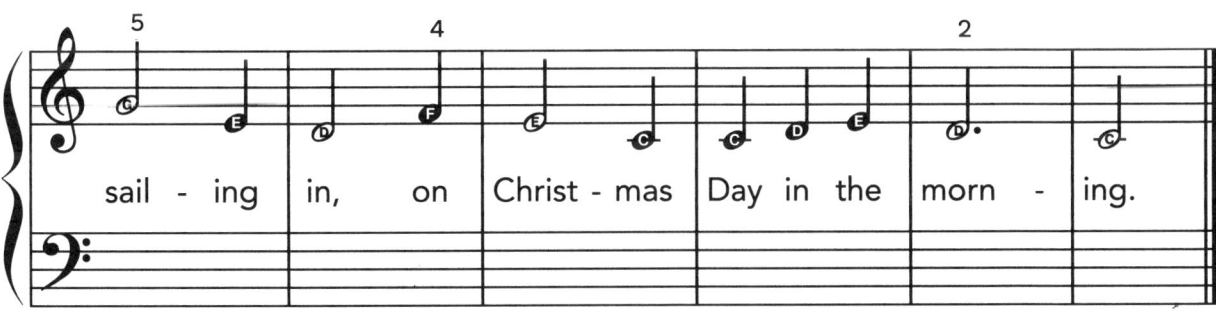

sail - ing in, on Christ - mas Day in the morn - ing.

Good King Wenceslas

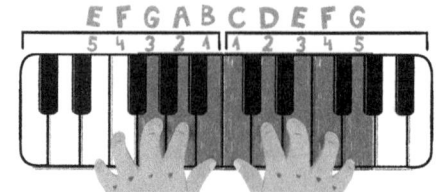

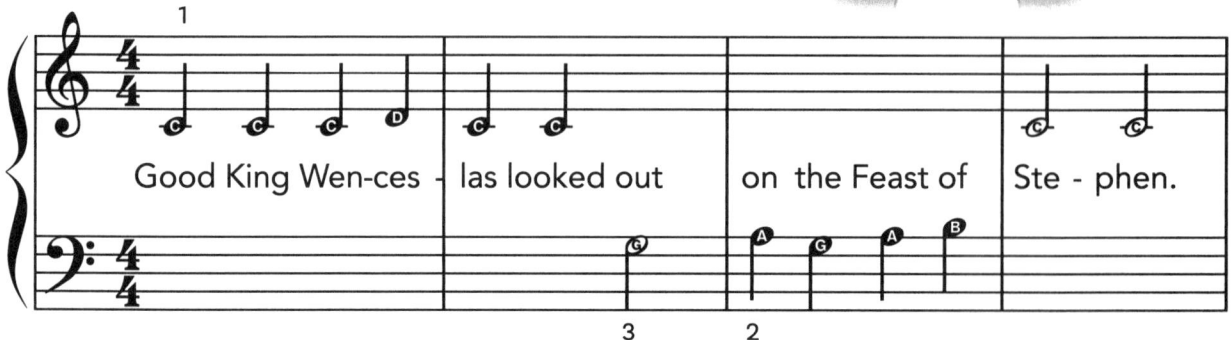

Good King Wen-ces - las looked out | on the Feast of | Ste - phen.

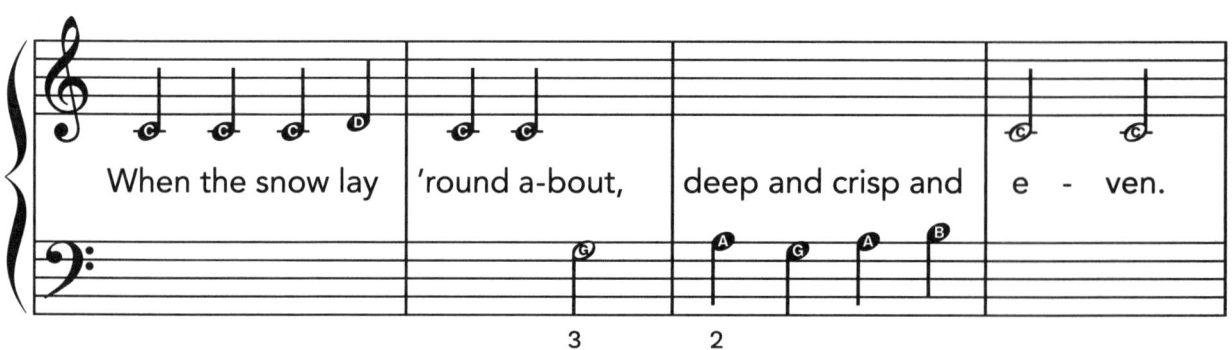

When the snow lay | 'round a-bout, | deep and crisp and | e - ven.

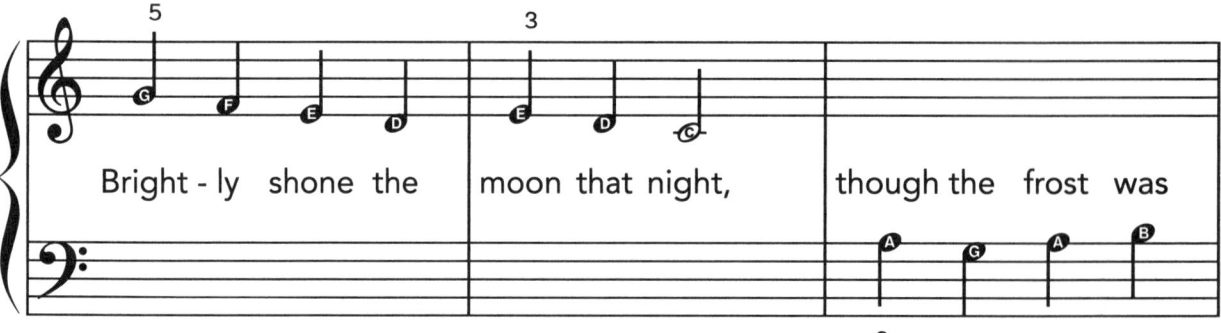

Bright - ly shone the | moon that night, | though the frost was

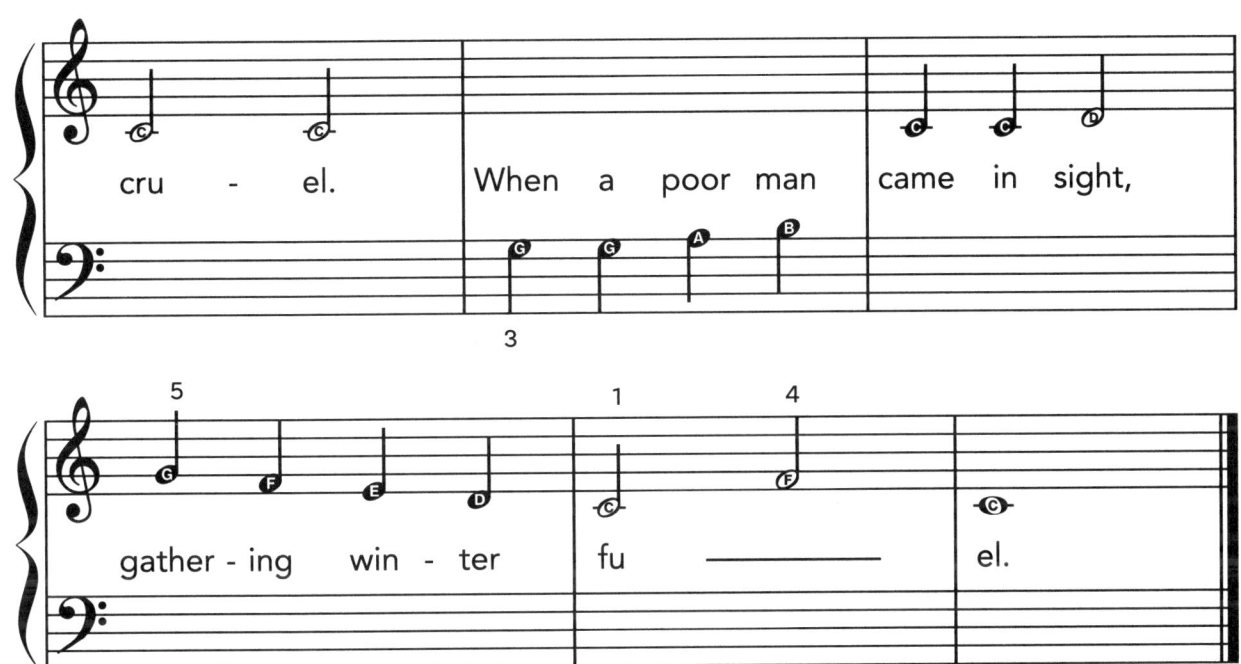

cru - el. When a poor man came in sight,

gather - ing win - ter fu ———— el.

O Christmas Tree

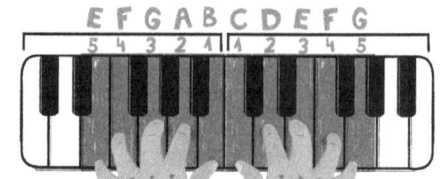

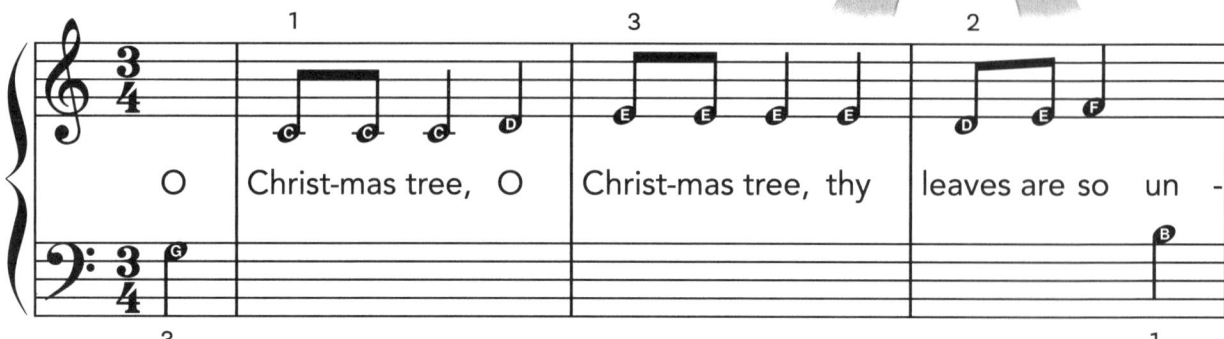

O Christ-mas tree, O Christ-mas tree, thy leaves are so un -

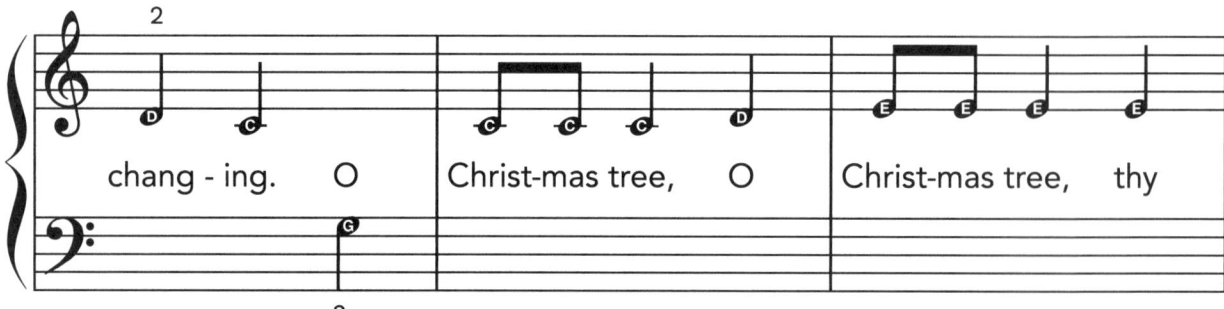

chang - ing. O Christ-mas tree, O Christ-mas tree, thy

leaves are so un - chang-ing. Not on-ly green when sum-mer's here, but

al - so when it's | cold and drear. O | Christ-mas tree, O

Christ-mas tree, thy | leaves are so un - | chang - ing.

Away in a Manger

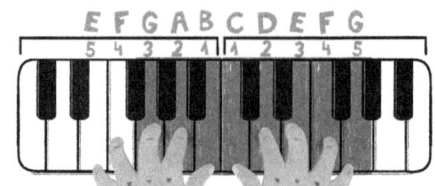

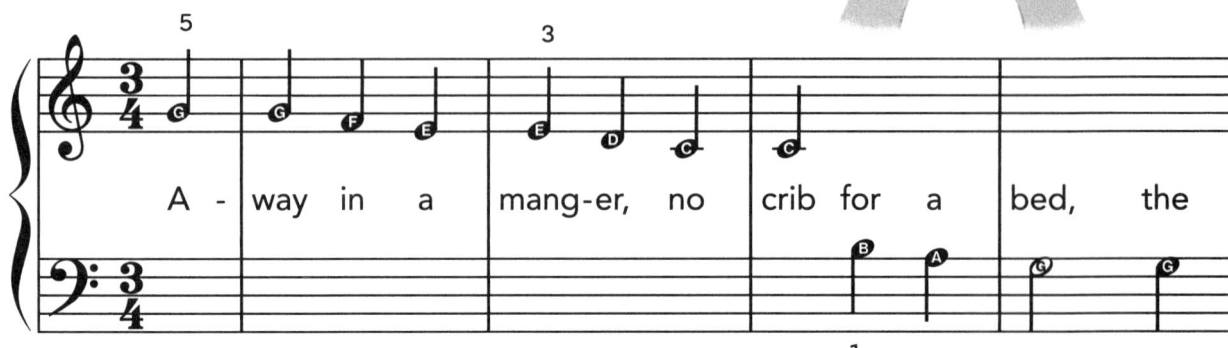

A - way in a mang-er, no crib for a bed, the

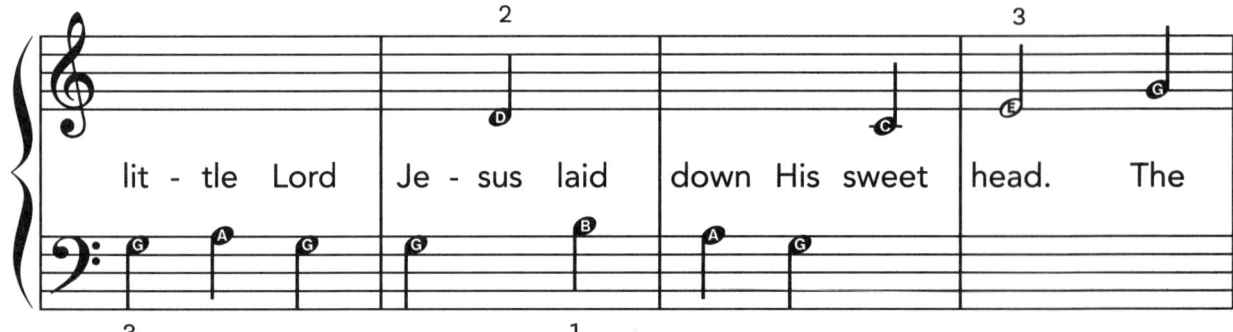

lit - tle Lord Je - sus laid down His sweet head. The

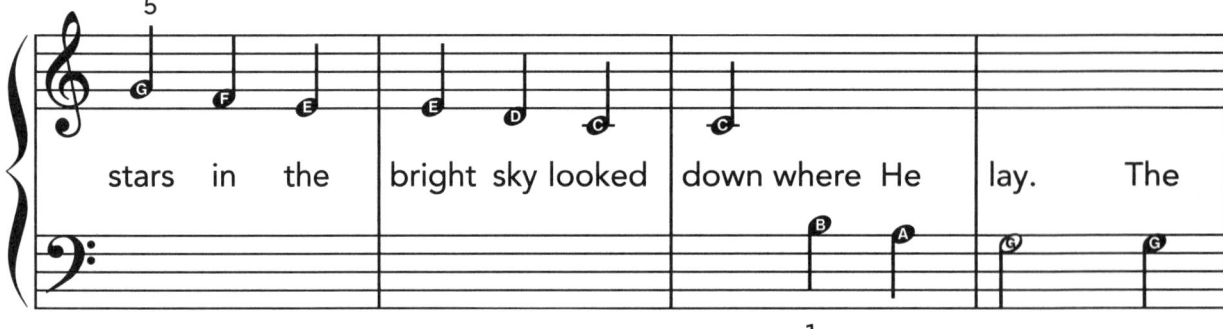

stars in the bright sky looked down where He lay. The

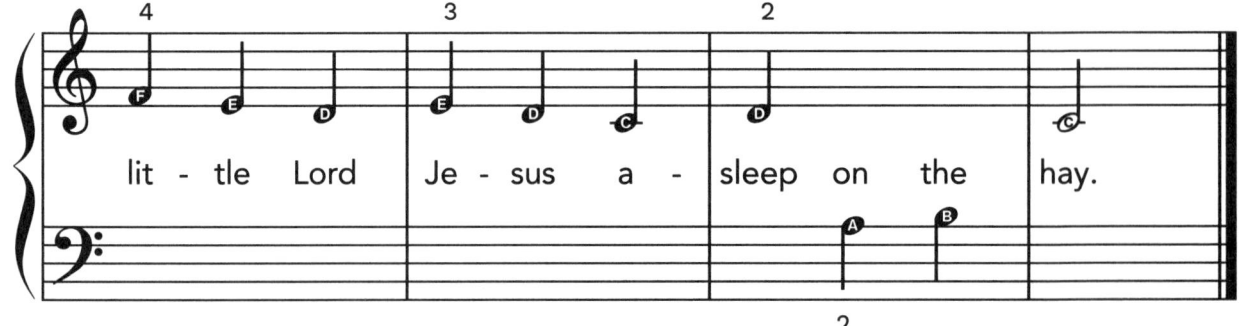

lit - tle Lord Je - sus a - sleep on the hay.

Go Tell It on the Mountain

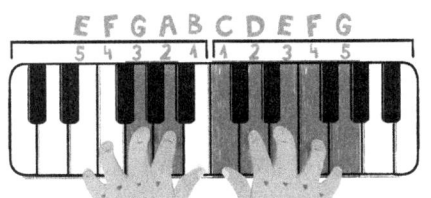

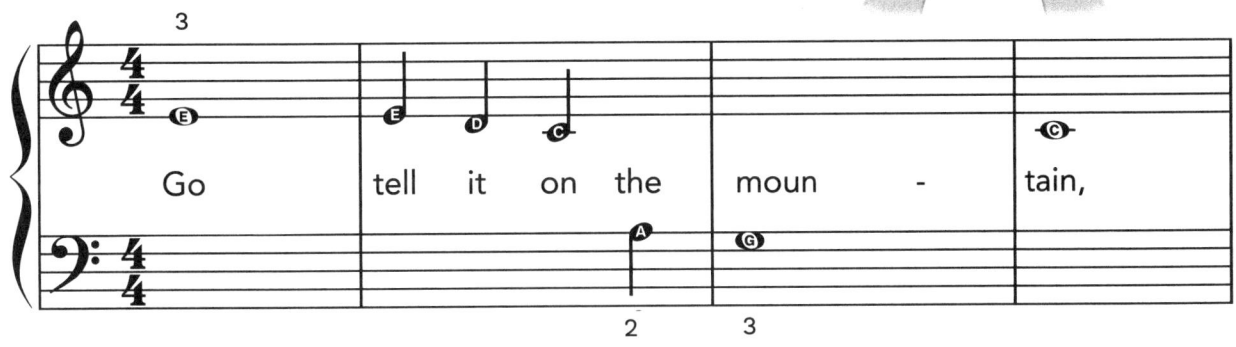

Go tell it on the moun - tain,

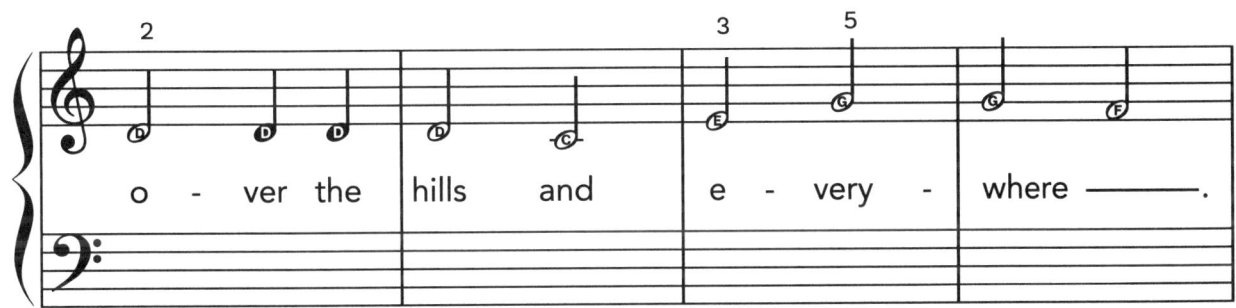

o - ver the hills and e - very - where ———.

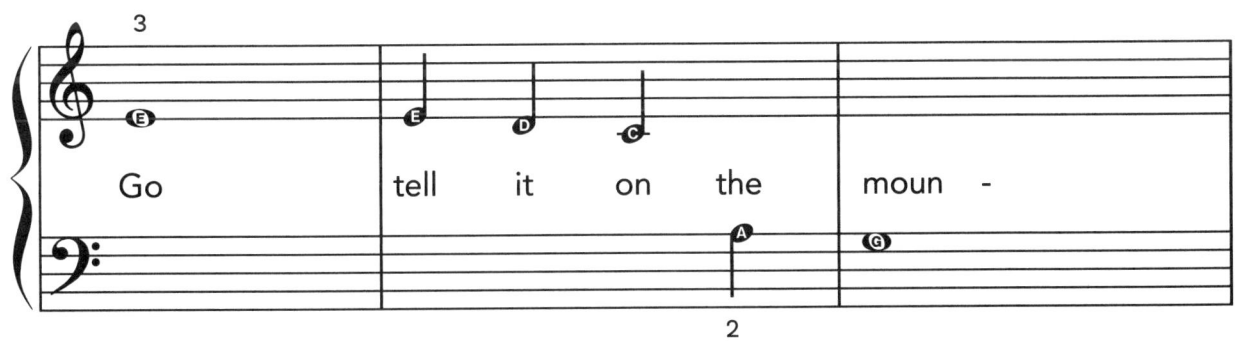

Go tell it on the moun -

tain that Je - sus Christ is born.

Ding Dong Merrily on High

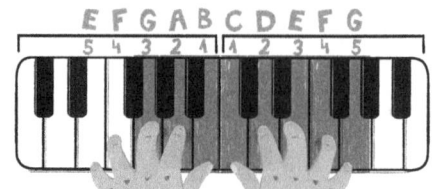

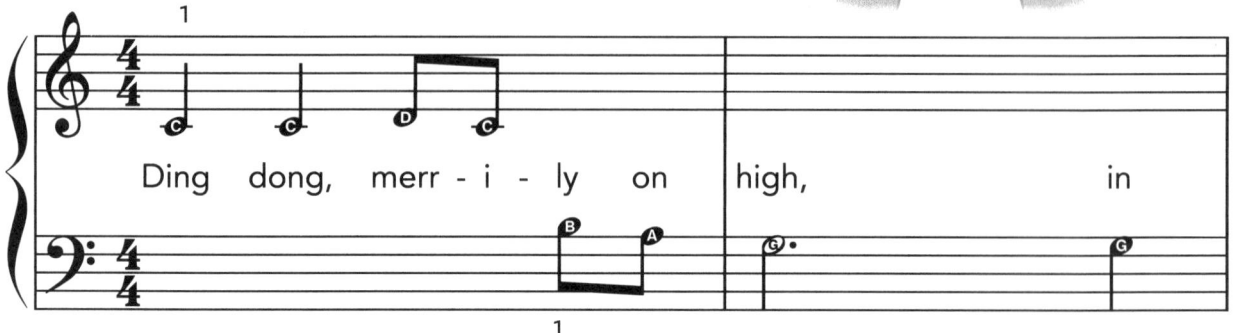

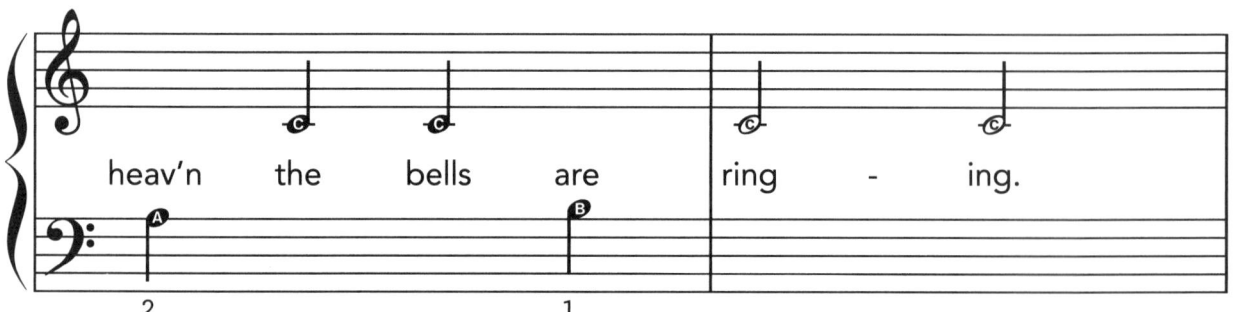

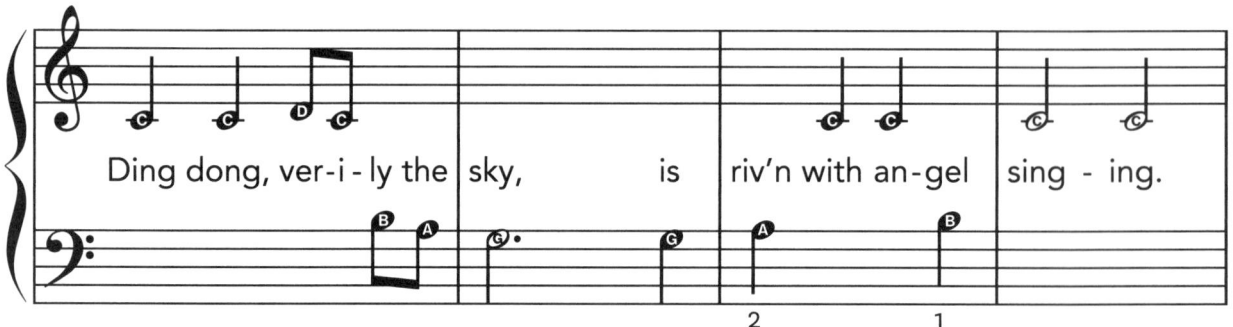

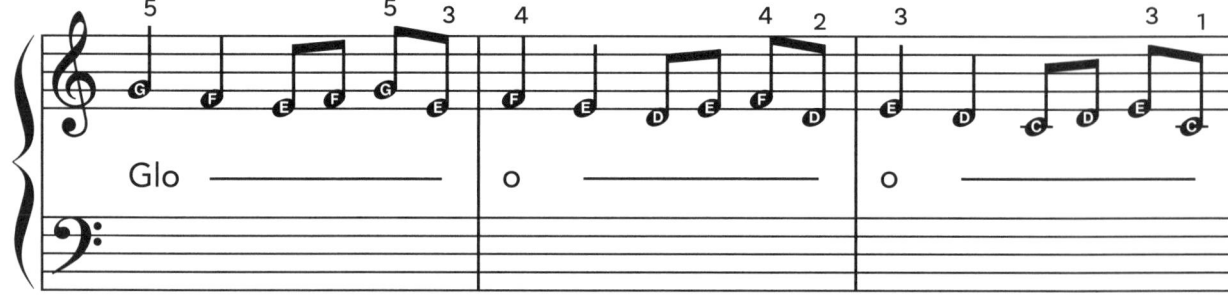

14

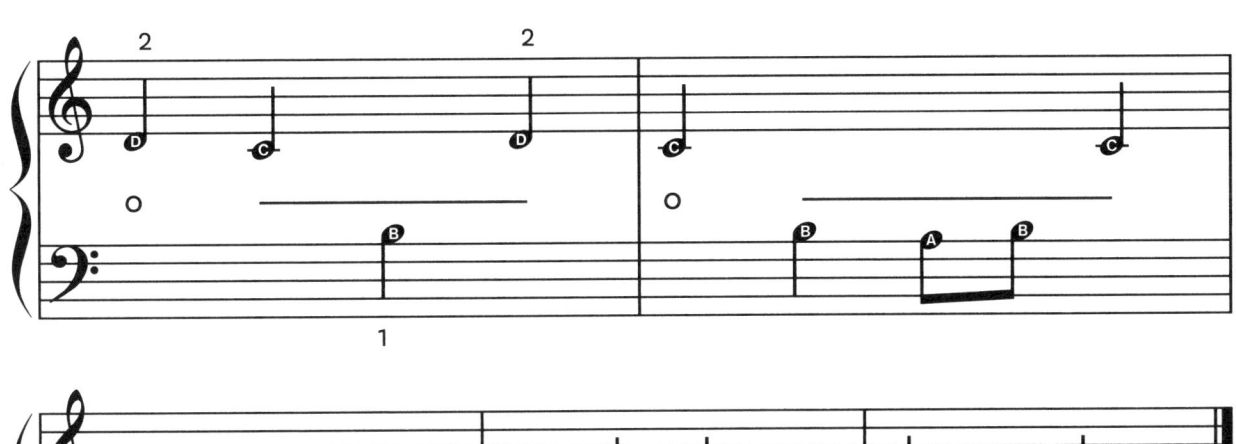

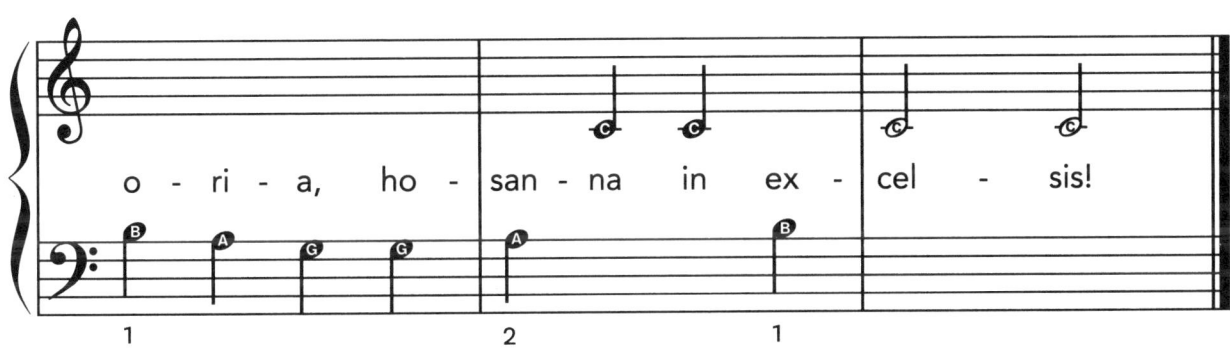

Up on the Housetop

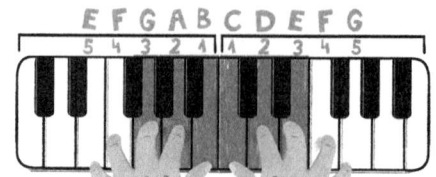

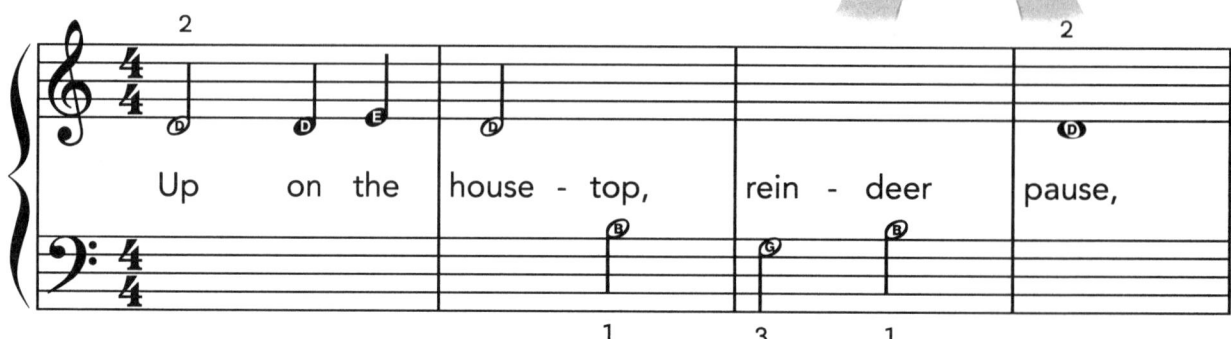

Up on the house-top, rein-deer pause,

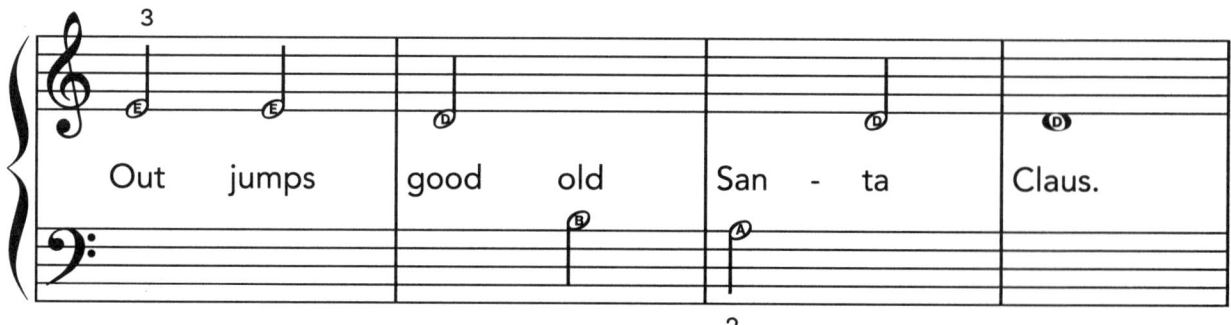

Out jumps good old San-ta Claus.

Down through the chim-ney with lots of toys,

all for the lit-tle ones' Christ-mas joys.

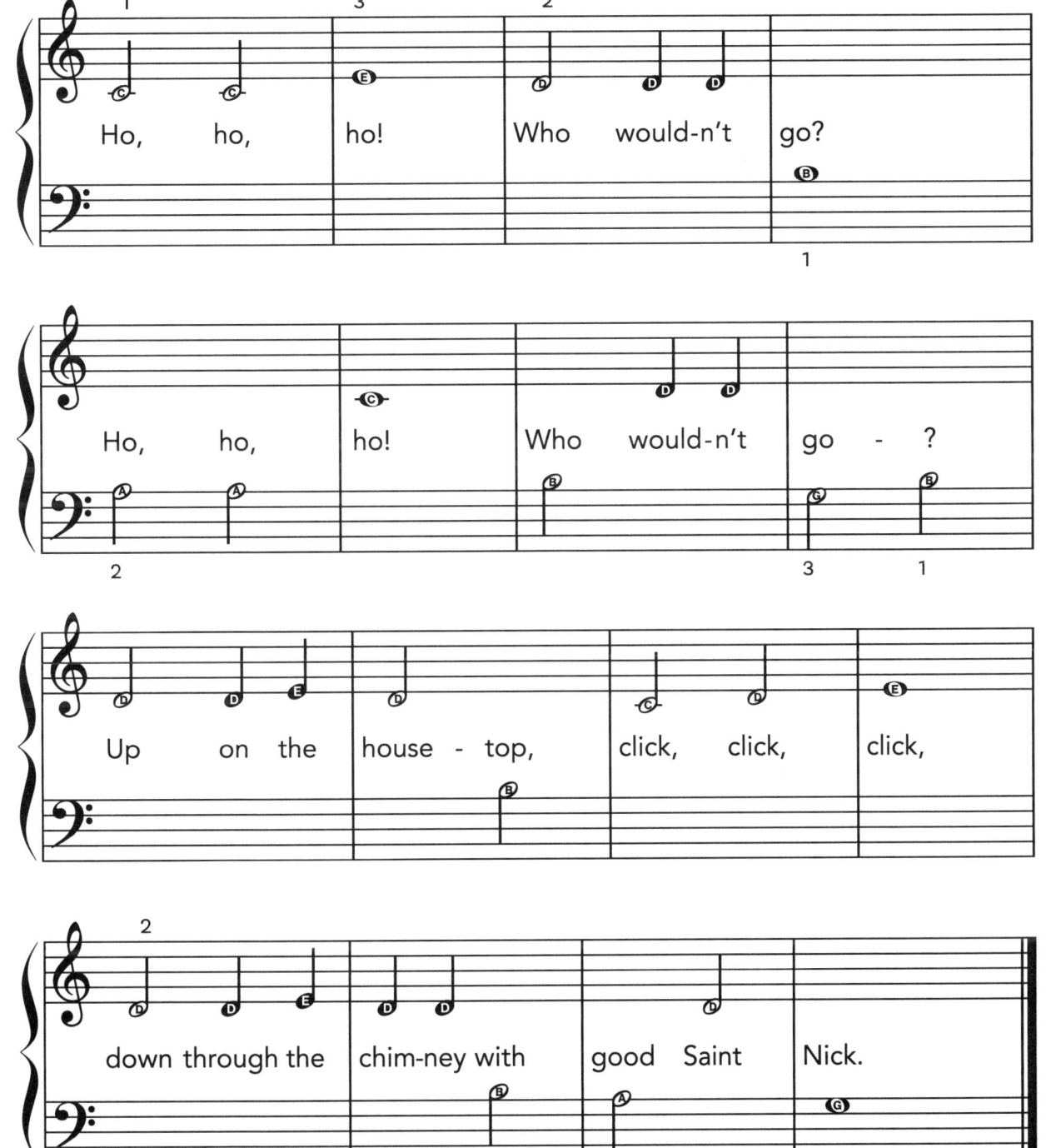

O Come, All Ye Faithful

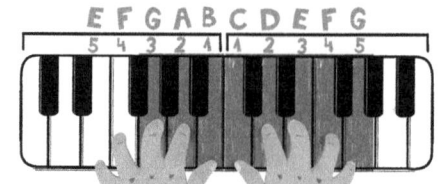

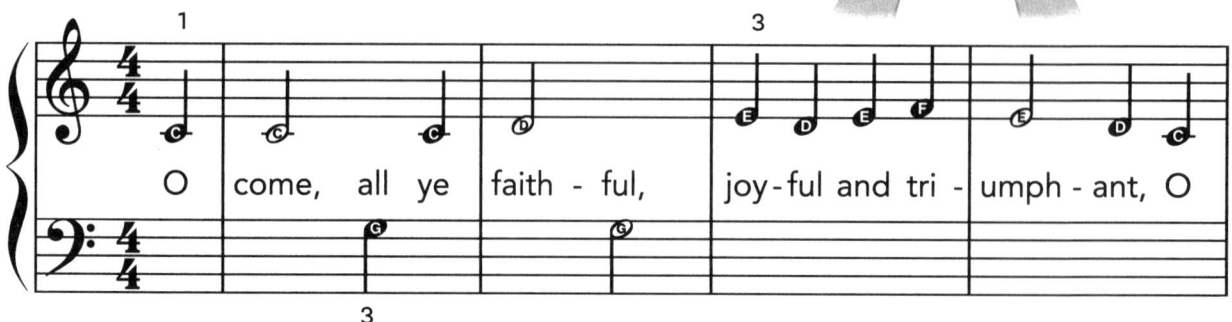

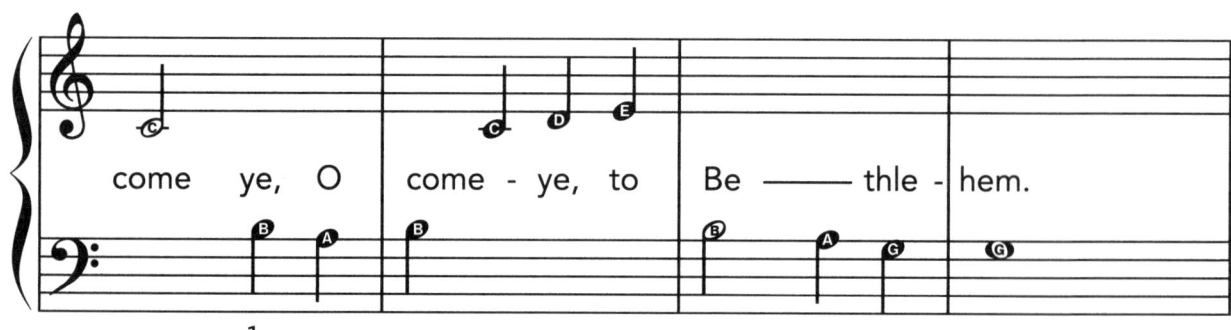

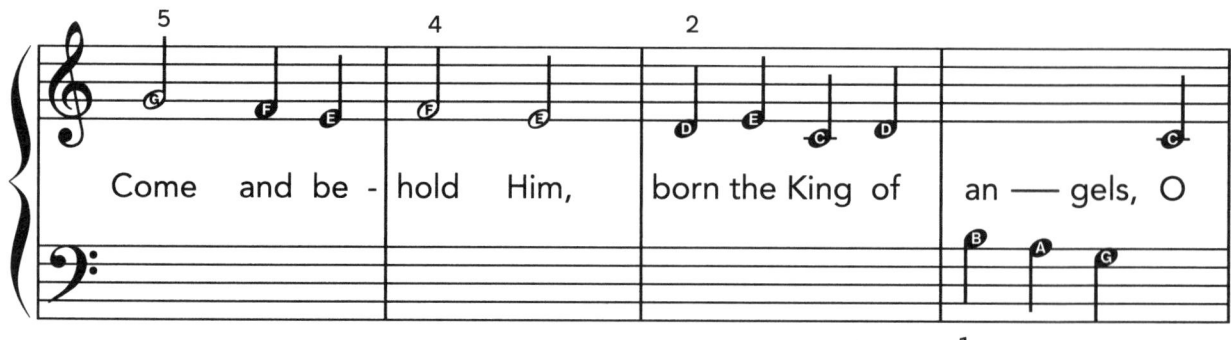

come let us a - dore Him, O come let us a - dore Him, O

come let us a - dore Him, - Christ - the Lord.

FUN FACT

The longest piano piece ever performed was called "Vexations" by Erik Satie. It was performed in 1963 by 12 different piano players and it took over 18 hours to perform!

O Come, O Come, Emmanuel

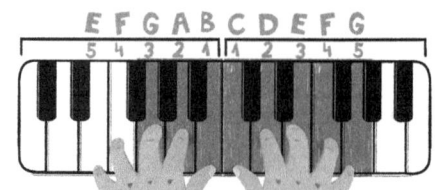

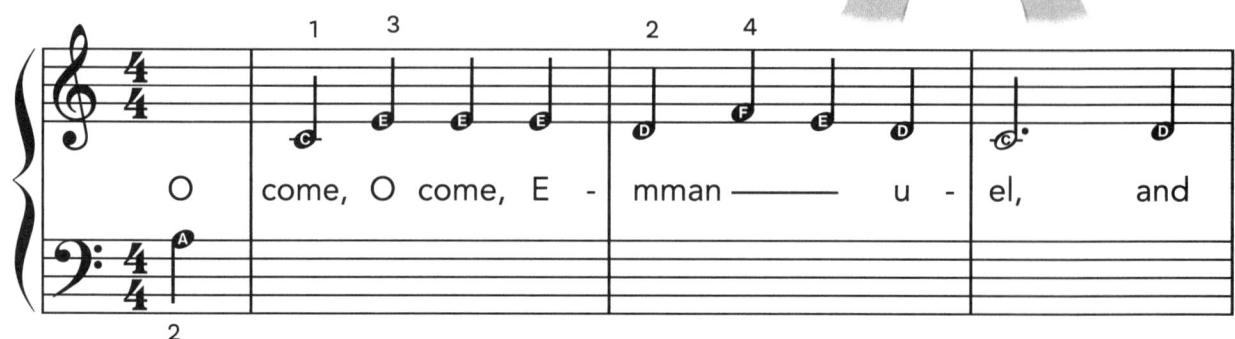

O come, O come, E - mman — — — u - el, and

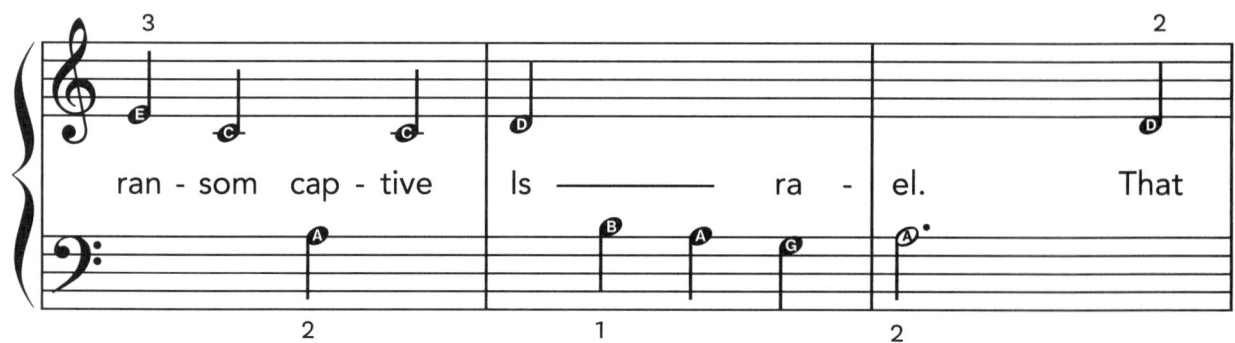

ran - som cap - tive Is — — — ra - el. That

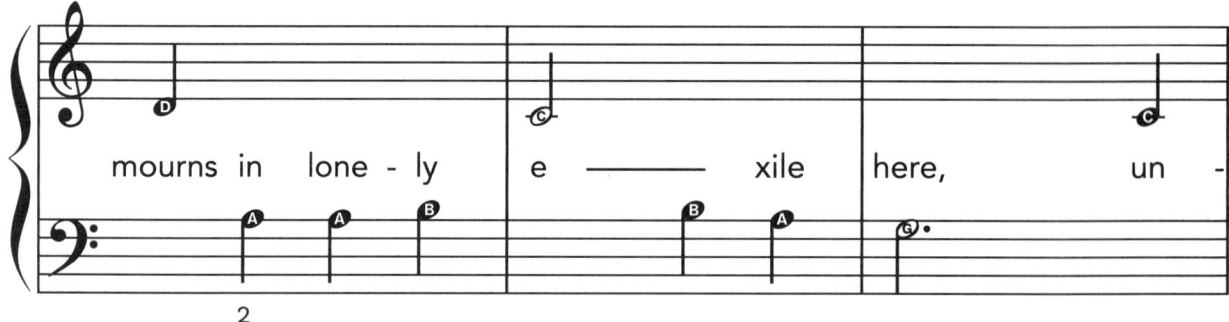

mourns in lone - ly e — — xile here, un -

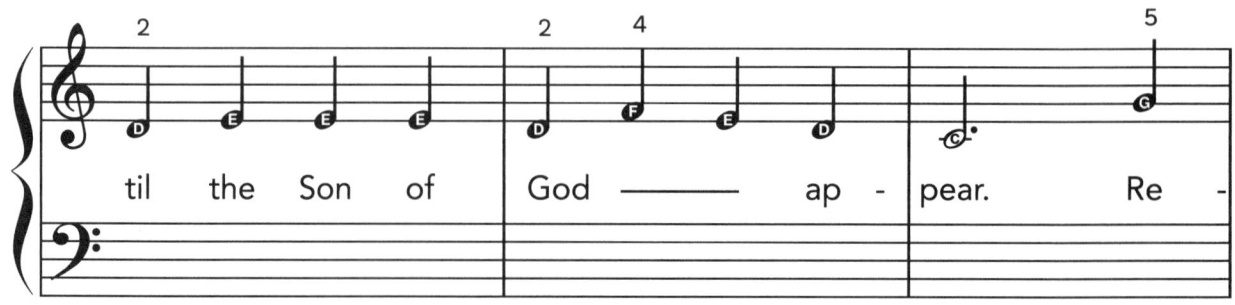

til the Son of God — — ap - pear. Re -

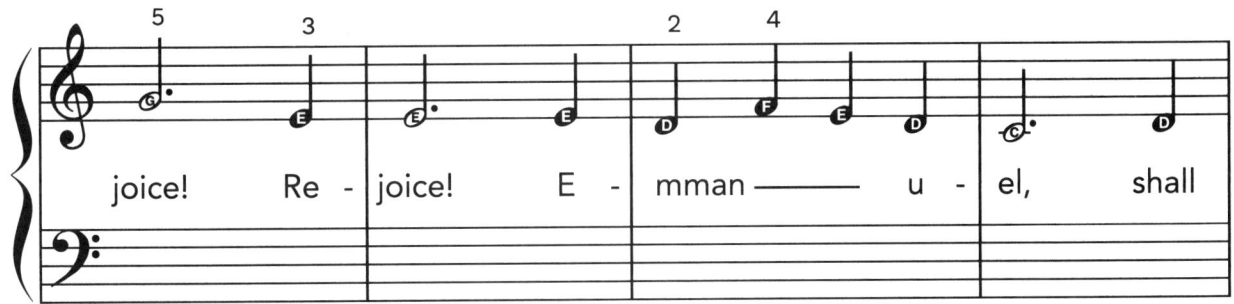

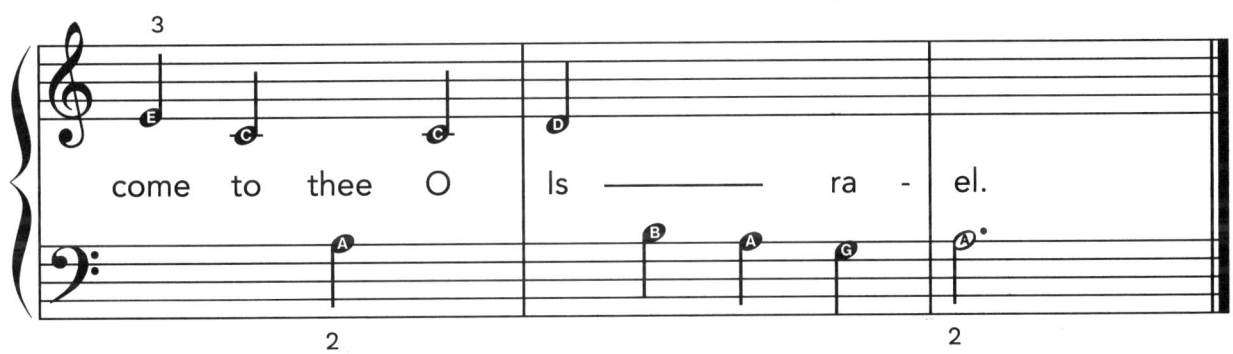

FUN FACT

In 2017, Domingos-Antonio Gomes set a world record by playing the "B7" key 824 times in 1 minute! This makes him the fastest piano player in the world.

We Wish You a Merry Christmas

We wish you a mer - ry Christ - mas, we

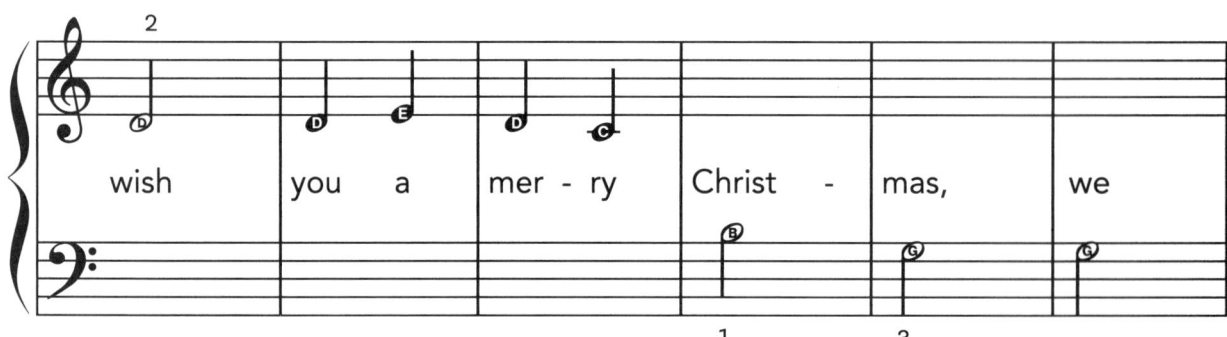

wish you a mer - ry Christ - mas, we

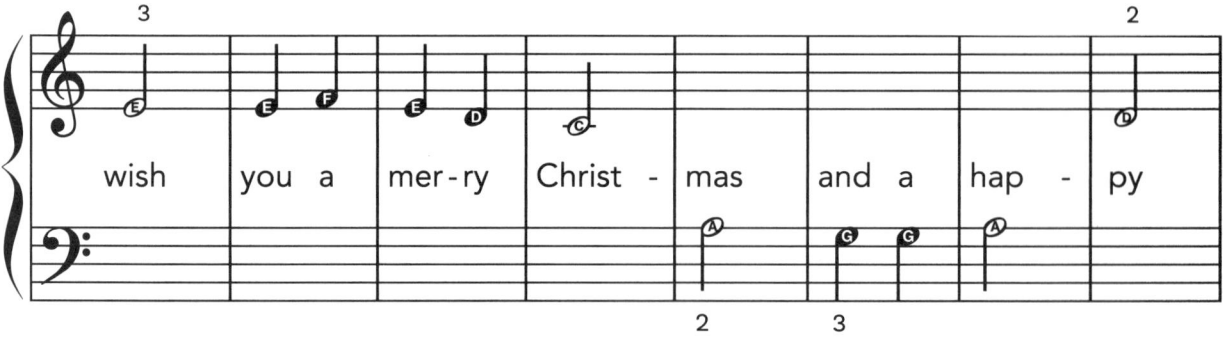

wish you a mer - ry Christ - mas and a hap - py

new year! Good ti - dings we bring to

continued

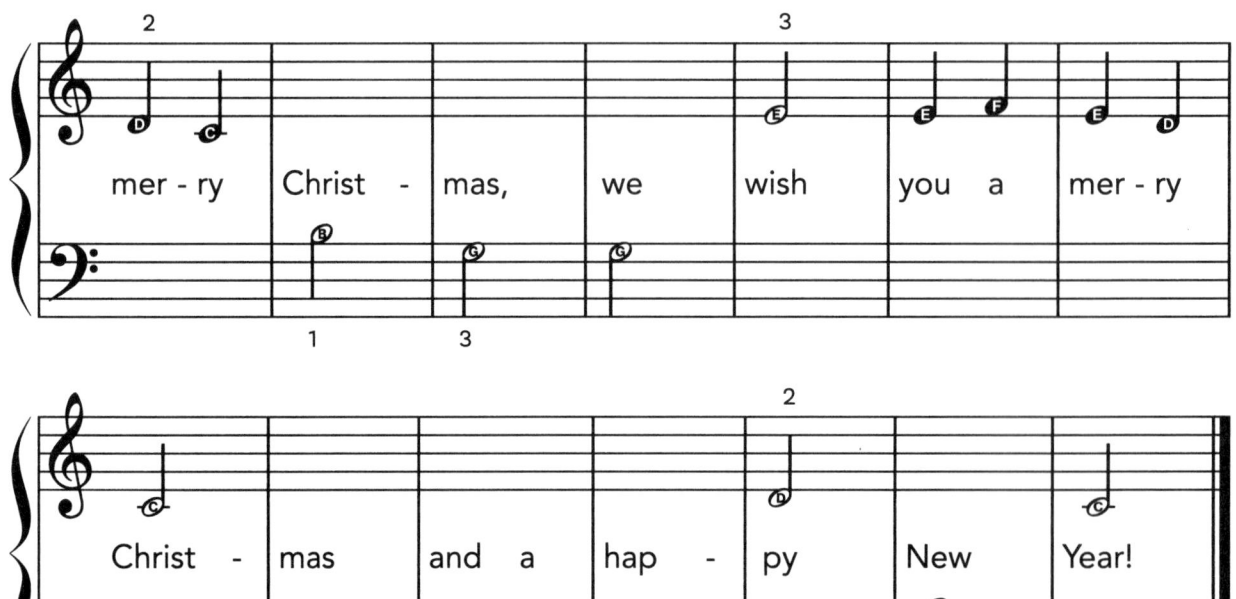

It Came Upon a Midnight Clear

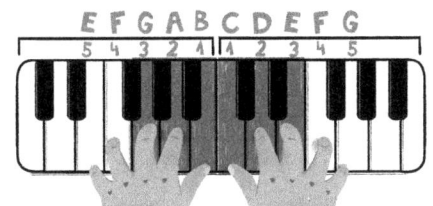

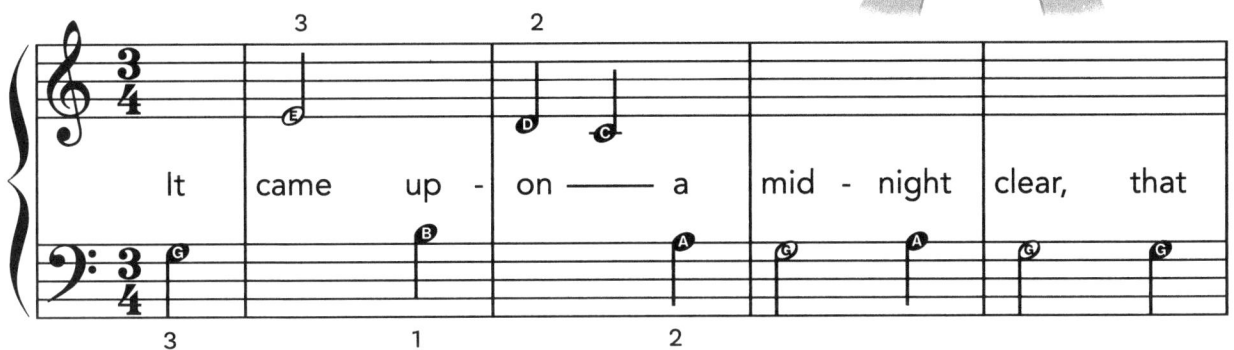

It came up - on —— a mid - night clear, that

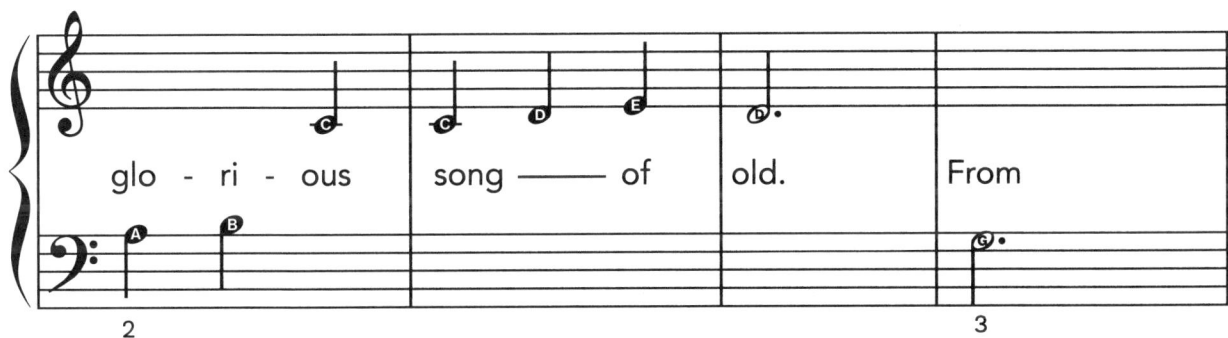

glo - ri - ous song —— of old. From

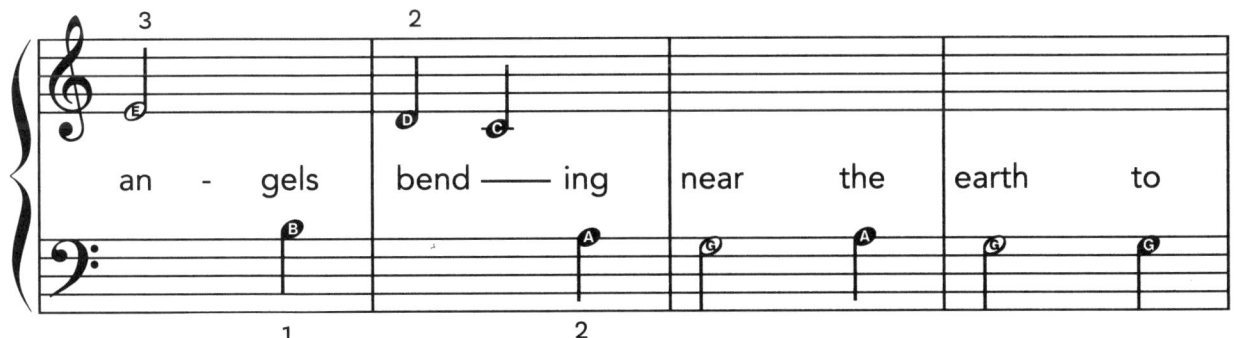

an - gels bend —— ing near the earth to

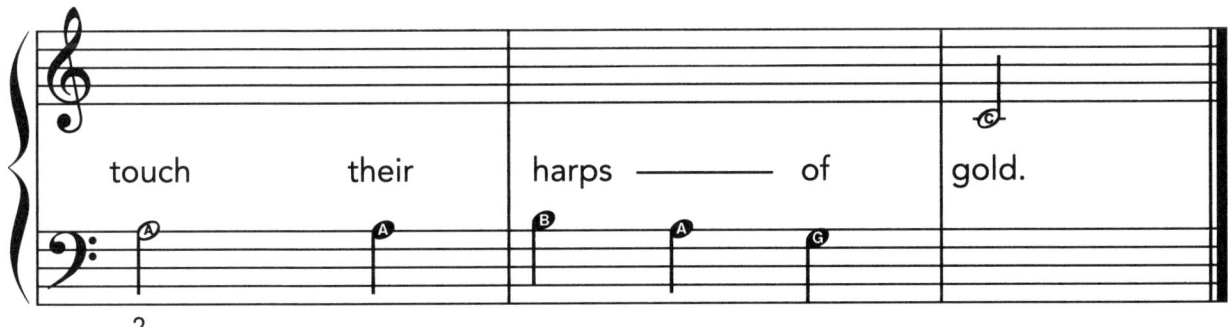

touch their harps —— of gold.

We Three Kings

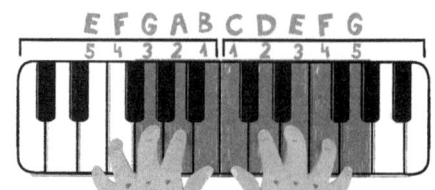

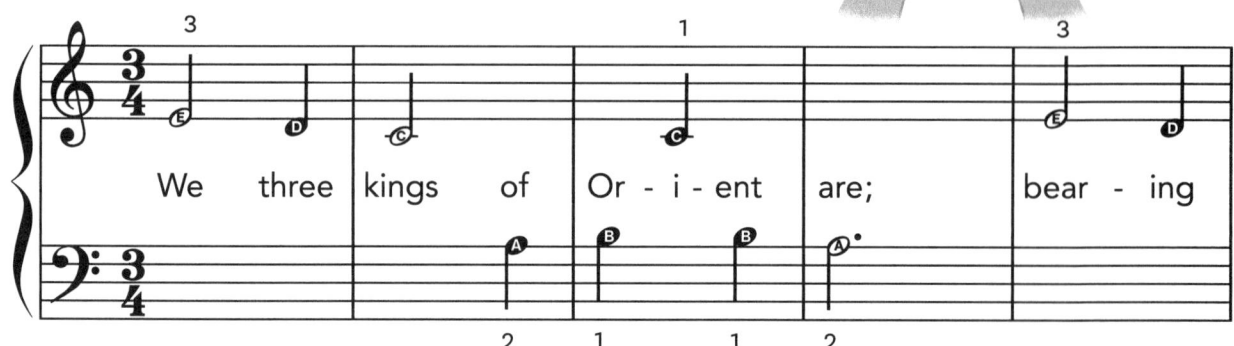

We three kings of Or - i - ent are; bear - ing

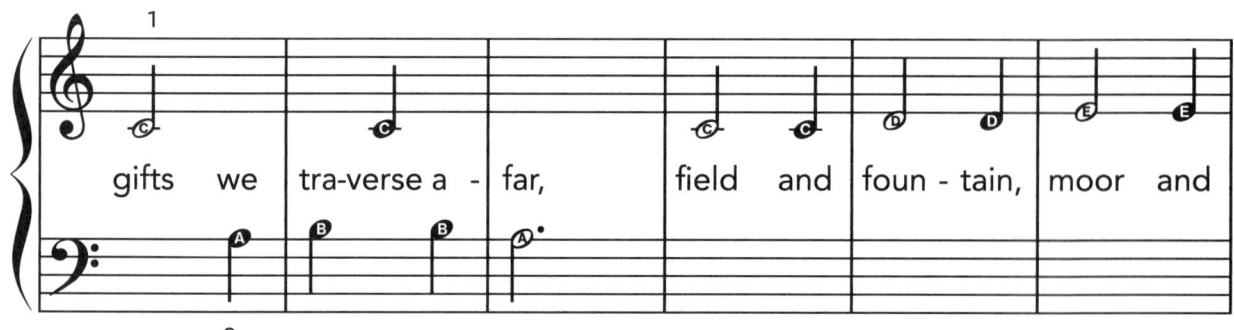

gifts we tra-verse a - far, field and foun - tain, moor and

moun — tain fol - low - ing yon - der star. O ——

star of won - der, star of night, star with roy - al

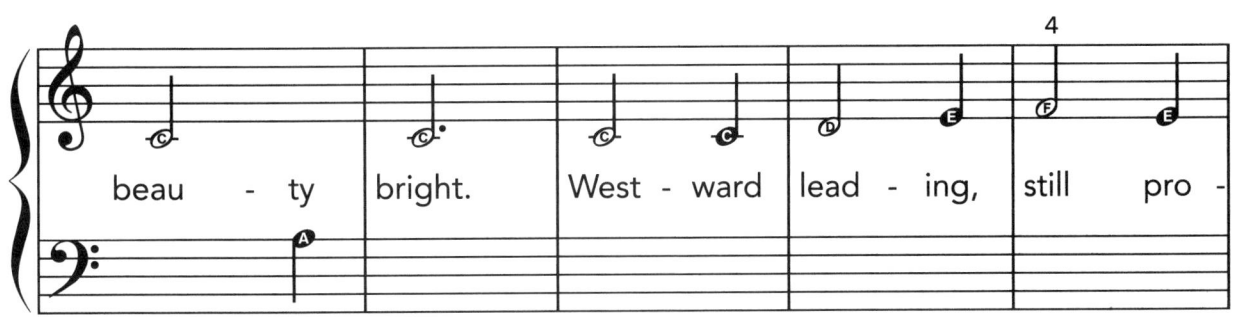

beau - ty bright. West - ward lead - ing, still pro -

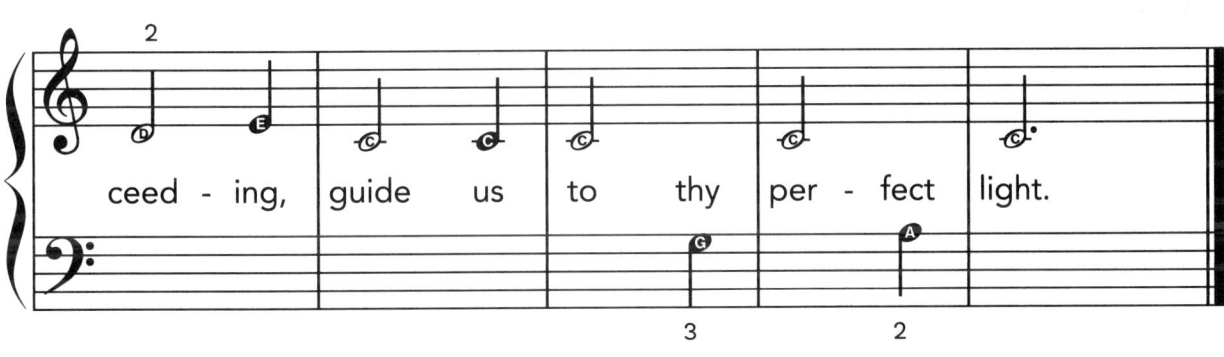

ceed - ing, guide us to thy per - fect light.

Angels We Have Heard on High

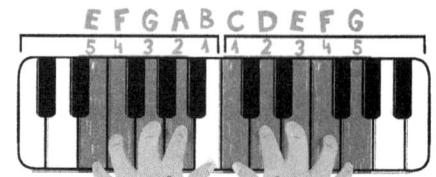

An-gels we have | heard on high, | sweet-ly sing-ing | o'er the plains.

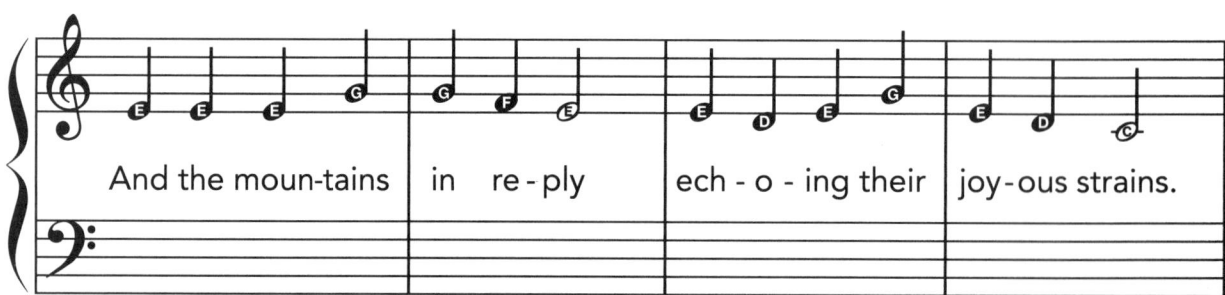

And the moun-tains | in re-ply | ech-o-ing their | joy-ous strains.

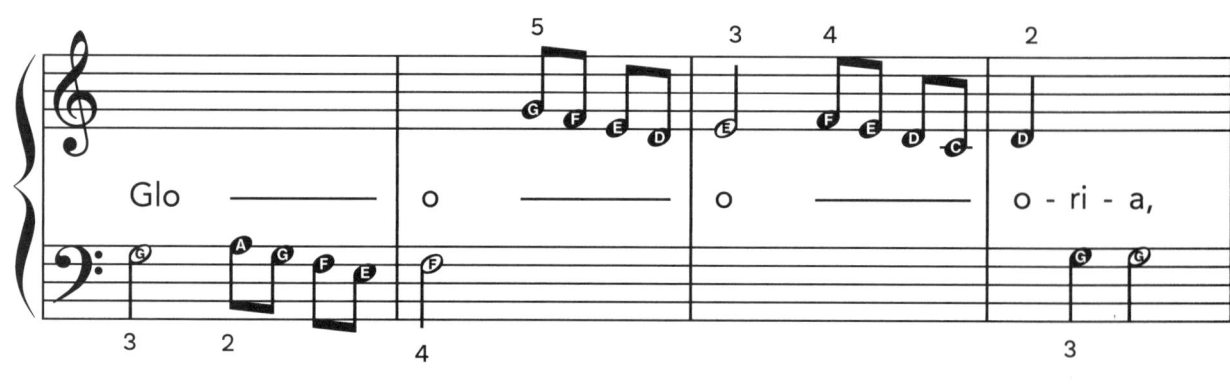

Glo ———— o ———— o ———— o-ri-a,

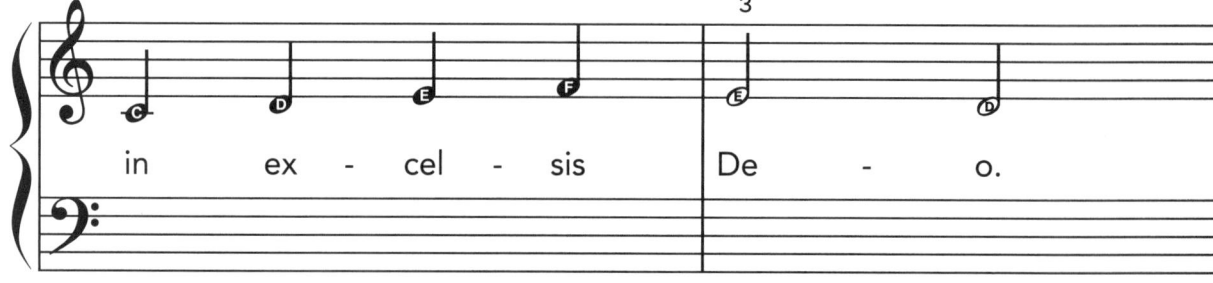

in ex - cel - sis De - o.

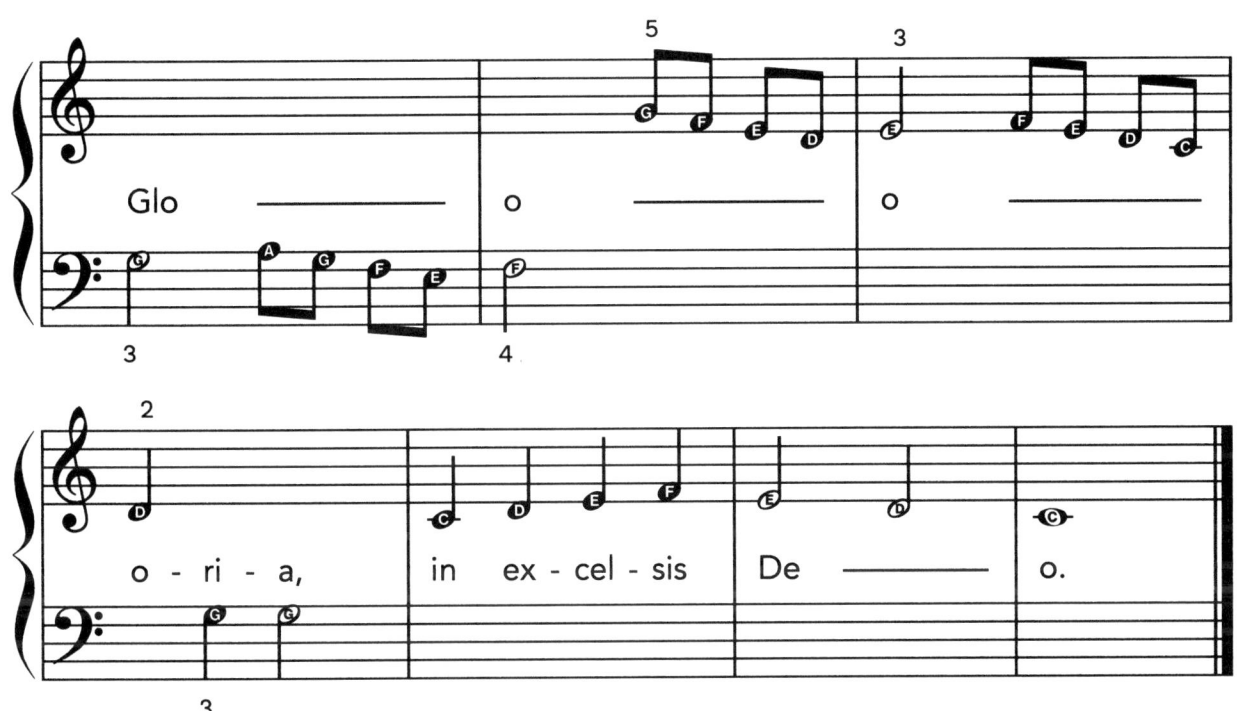

Glo ——— o ——— o ———
o - ri - a, in ex - cel - sis De ——— o.

Hark! the Herald Angels Sing

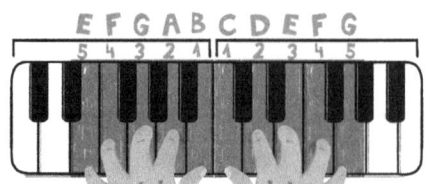

E F G A B C D E F G
5 4 3 2 1 1 2 3 4 5

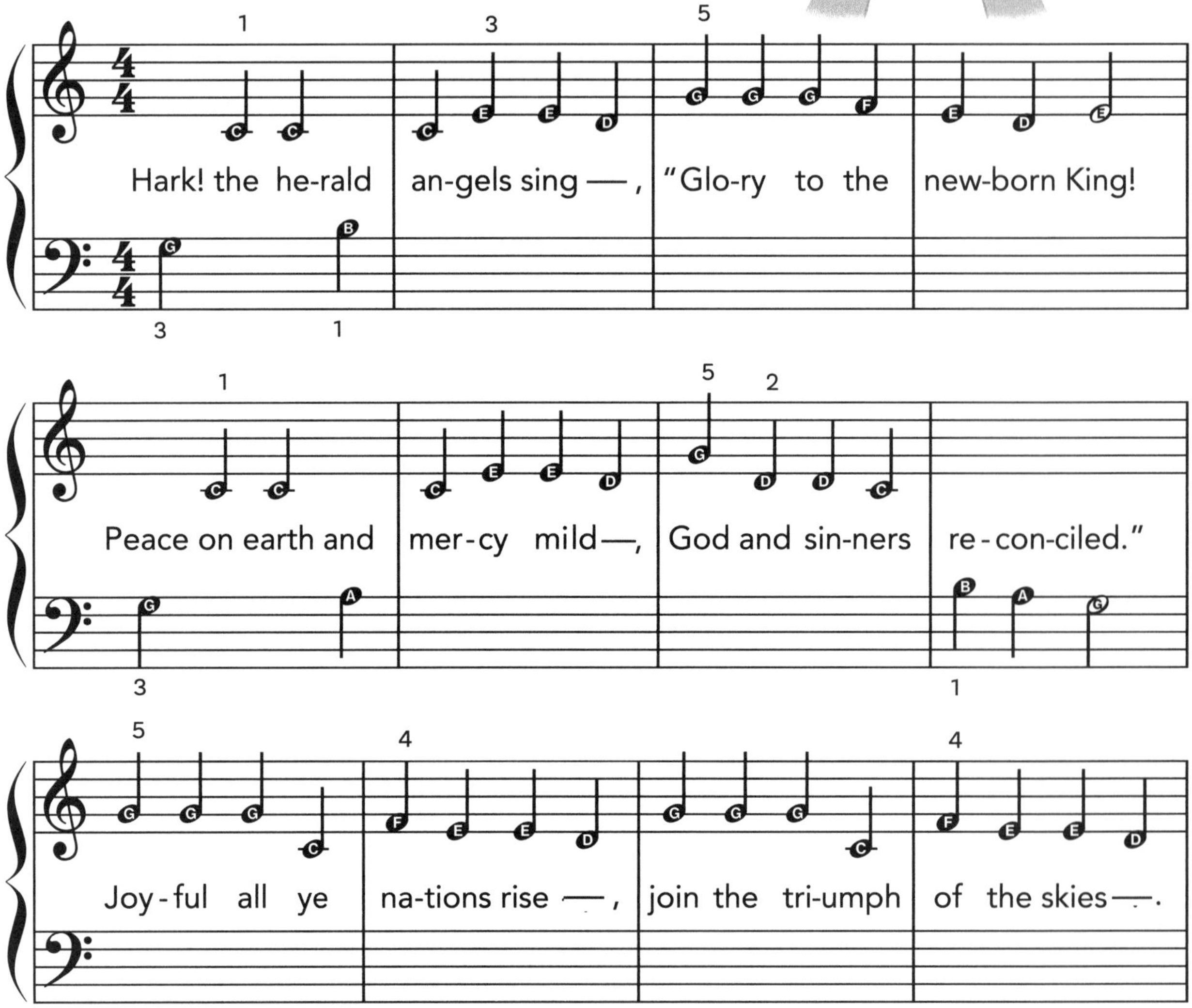
Hark! the he-rald an-gels sing —, "Glo-ry to the new-born King!
Peace on earth and mer-cy mild—, God and sin-ners re-con-ciled."
Joy-ful all ye na-tions rise —, join the tri-umph of the skies—.

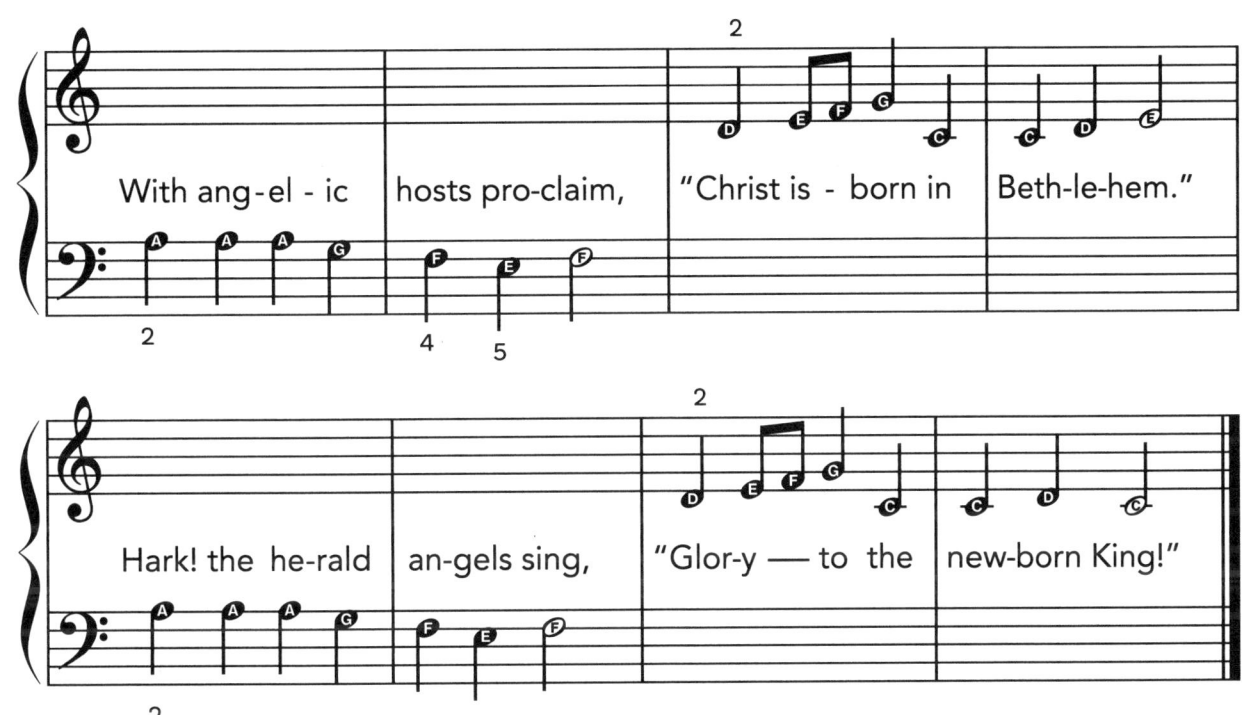

With ang-el-ic | hosts pro-claim, | "Christ is - born in | Beth-le-hem."

Hark! the he-rald | an-gels sing, | "Glor-y — to the | new-born King!"

Silent Night

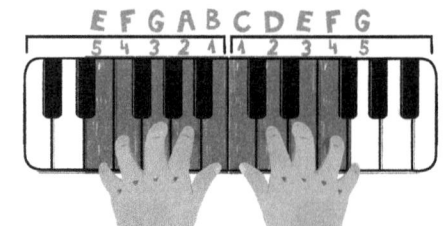

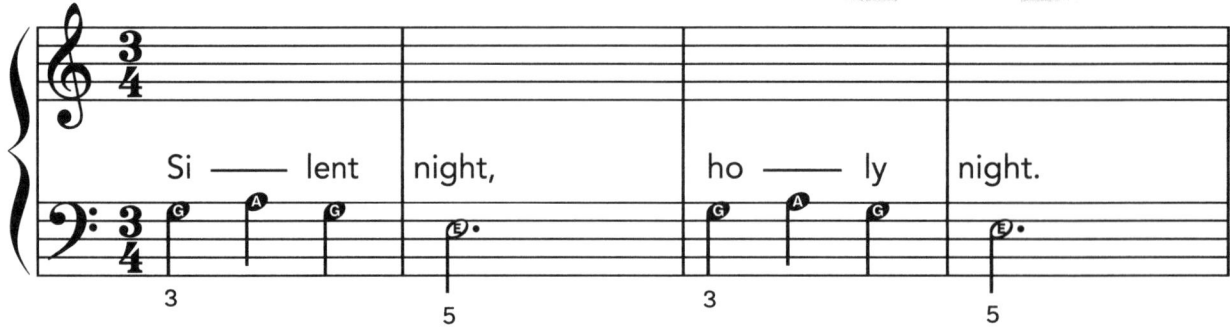

Si —— lent night, ho —— ly night.

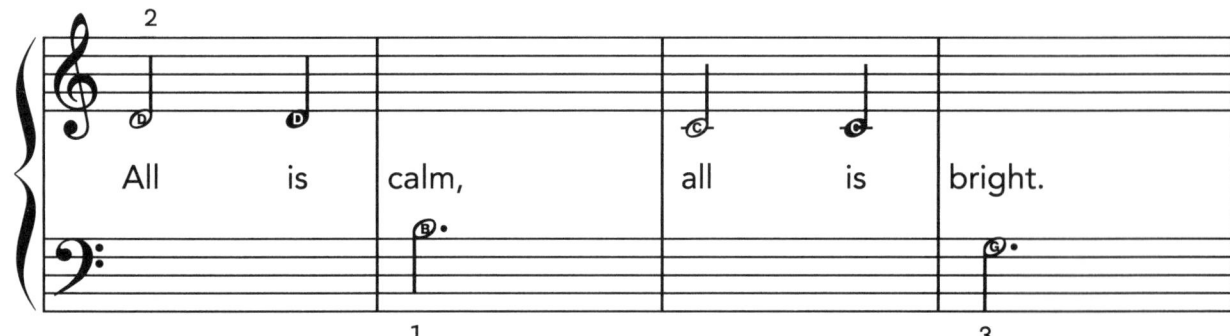

All is calm, all is bright.

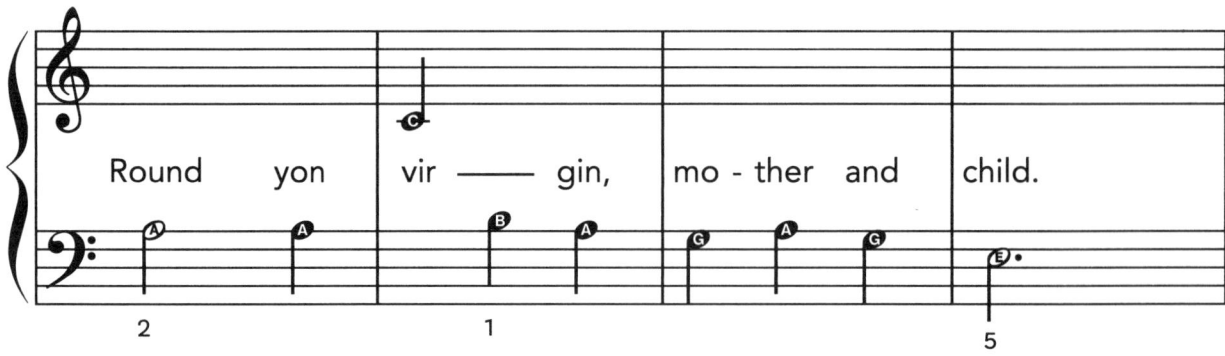

Round yon vir —— gin, mo - ther and child.

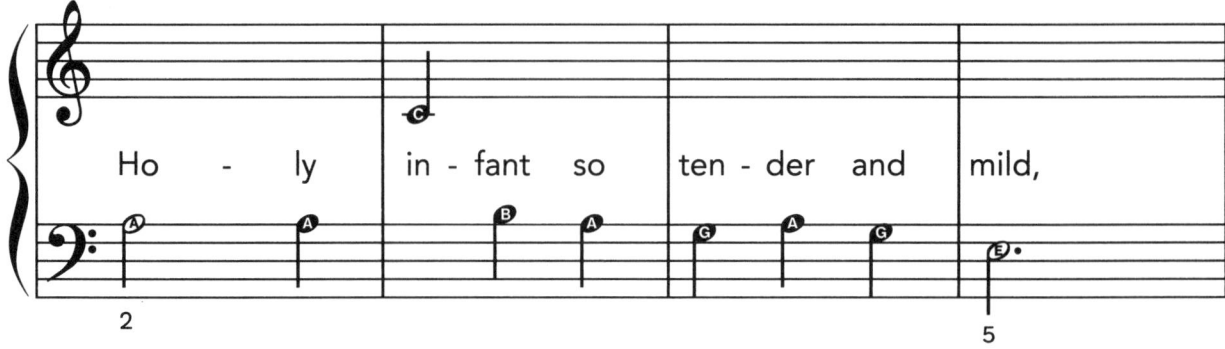

Ho - ly in - fant so ten - der and mild,

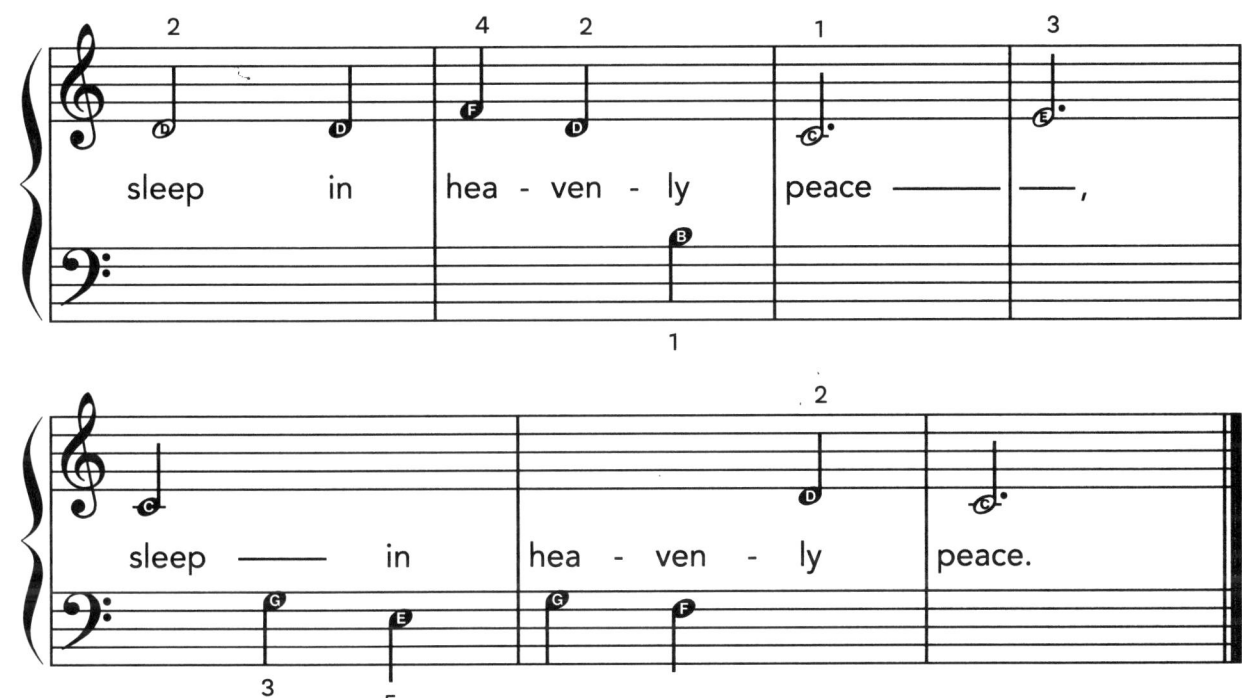

FUN FACT

"Silent Night" was written in 1818 and was first performed in Austria on Christmas Eve. It has been recorded over 100,000 times, making it the most recorded Christmas song ever!

Here We Come A-Caroling

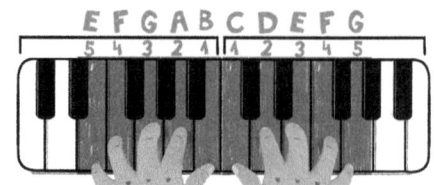

Here we come a - car - ol - ing a - mong the leaves so green,

here we come a - wand - 'ring so fair —— to be seen. Love and

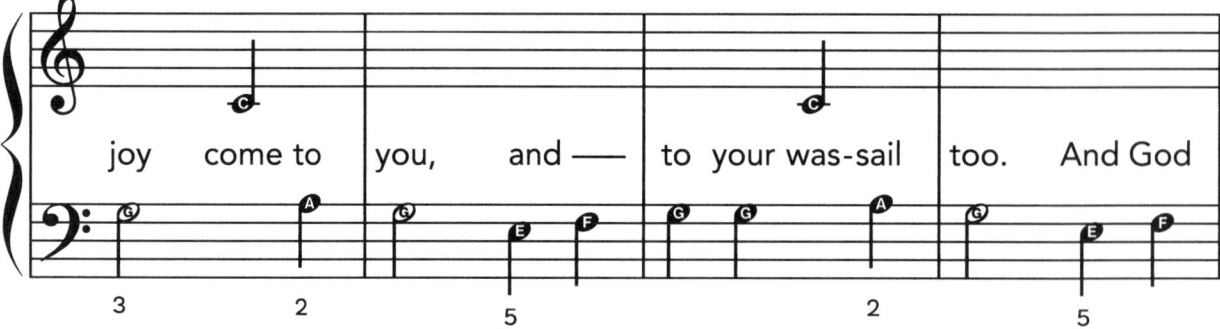

joy come to you, and —— to your was-sail too. And God

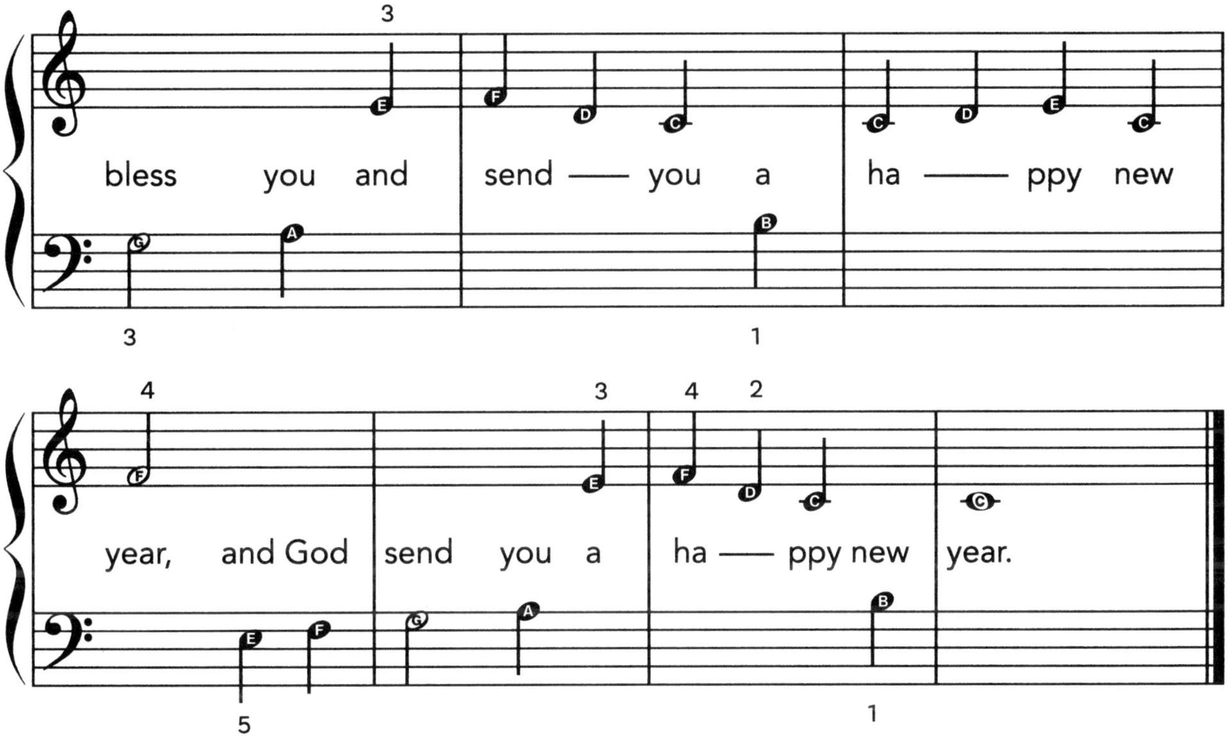

Staff line 1:

bless   you and | send — you a | ha — ppy new

(notes: E, F, D, C, C, D, E, C; bass: G, A, B)

Staff line 2:

year,   and God | send   you a | ha — ppy new | year.

(notes: F, E, F, D, C, C; bass: E, F, G, A, B)

The First Noel

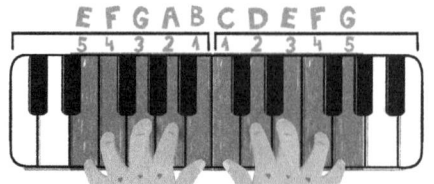

The— first — No— el the — an-gel did say was to

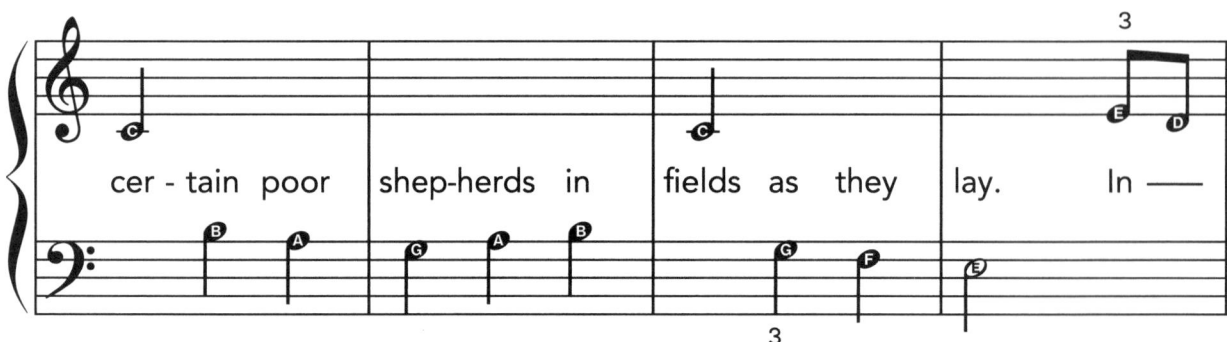

cer - tain poor shep-herds in fields as they lay. In —

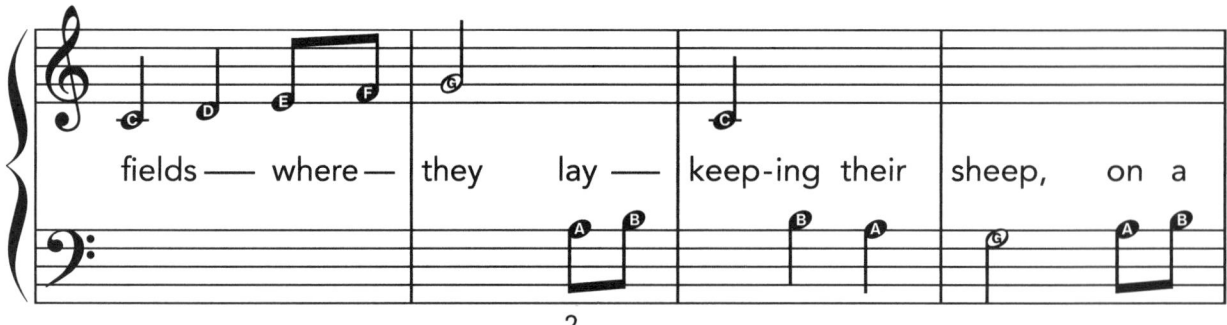

fields — where — they lay — keep-ing their sheep, on a

The Holly and the Ivy

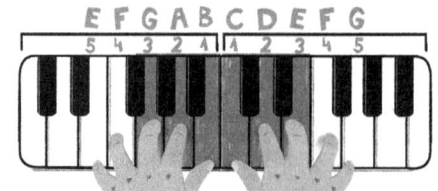

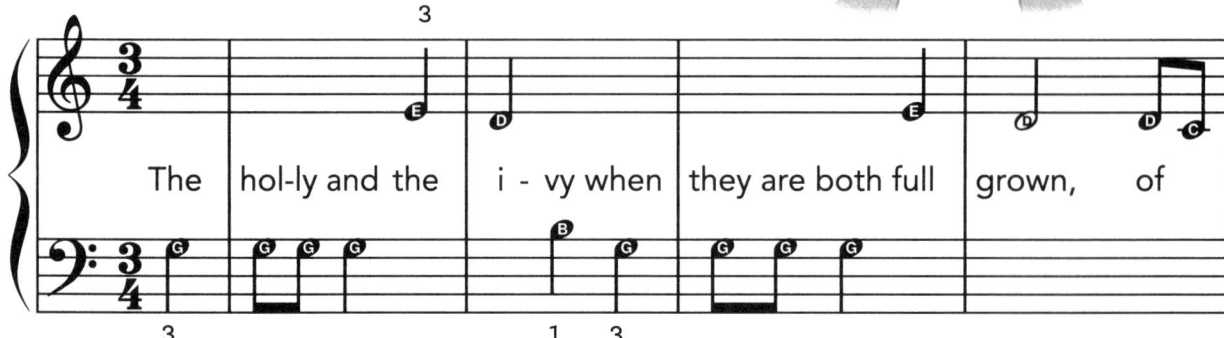

The | hol-ly and the | i - vy when | they are both full | grown, of

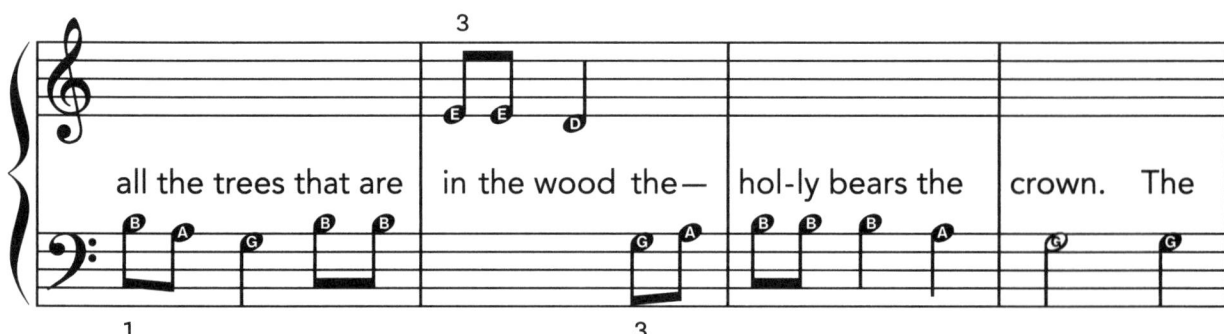

all the trees that are | in the wood the— | hol-ly bears the | crown. The

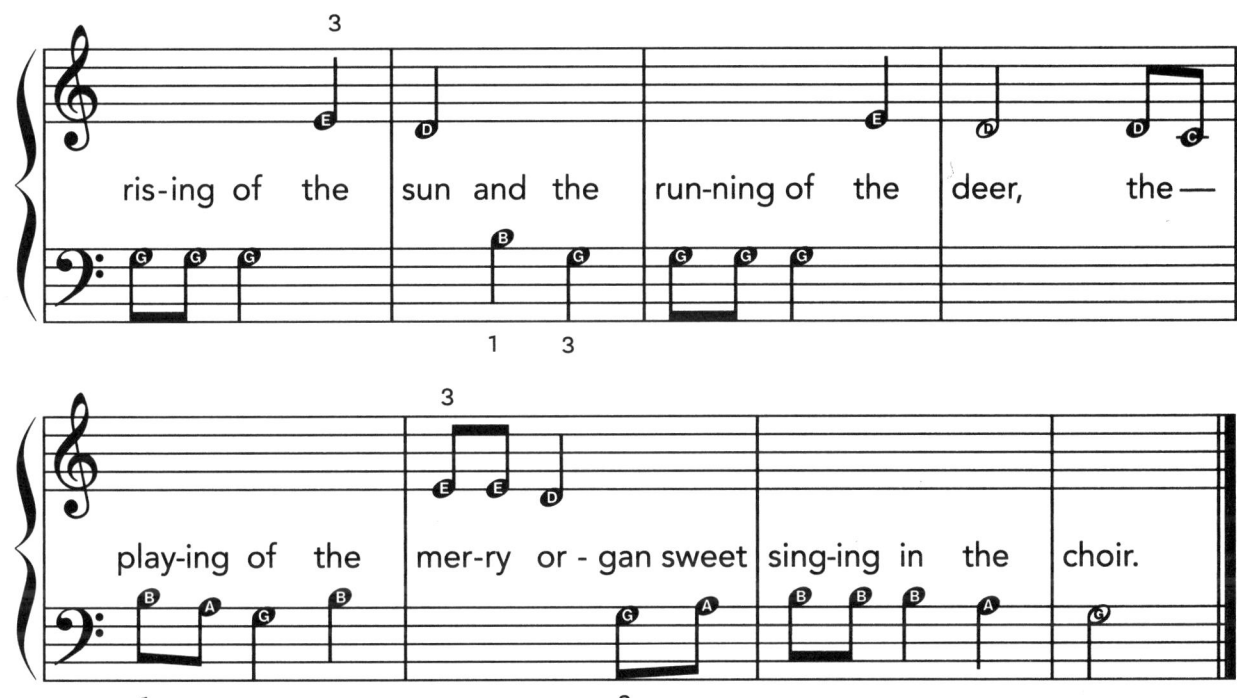

FUN FACT

Did you know that some pianos play themselves? Player pianos use special rolls of paper or modern technology to play music without anyone touching the keys!

Deck the Halls

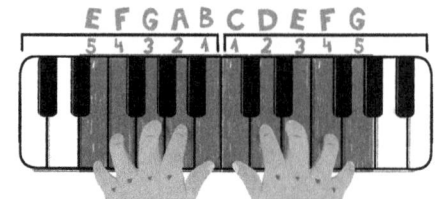

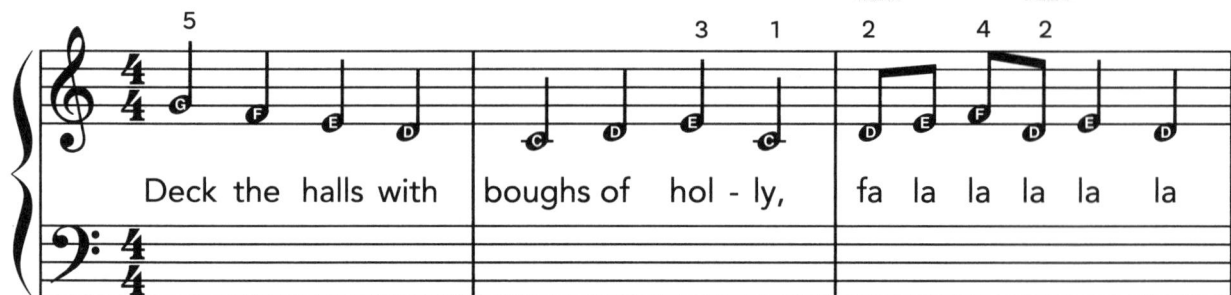

Deck the halls with | boughs of hol - ly, | fa la la la la la

la la la. | 'Tis the sea-son | to be jol - ly, | fa la la la la la

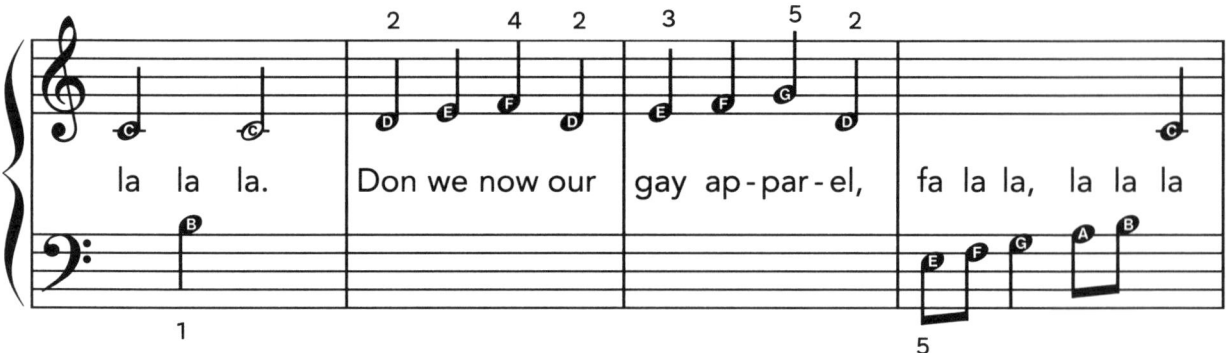

la la la. | Don we now our | gay ap-par-el, | fa la la, la la la

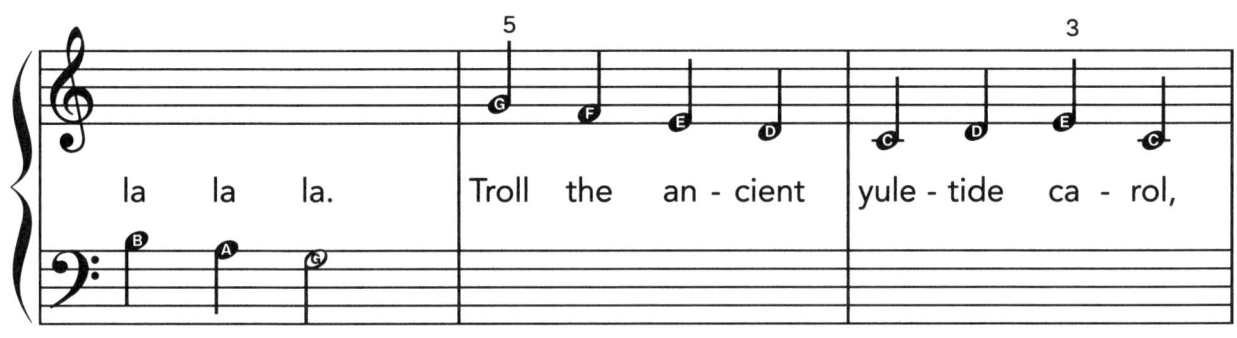

la   la   la.   Troll   the   an - cient   yule - tide   ca - rol,

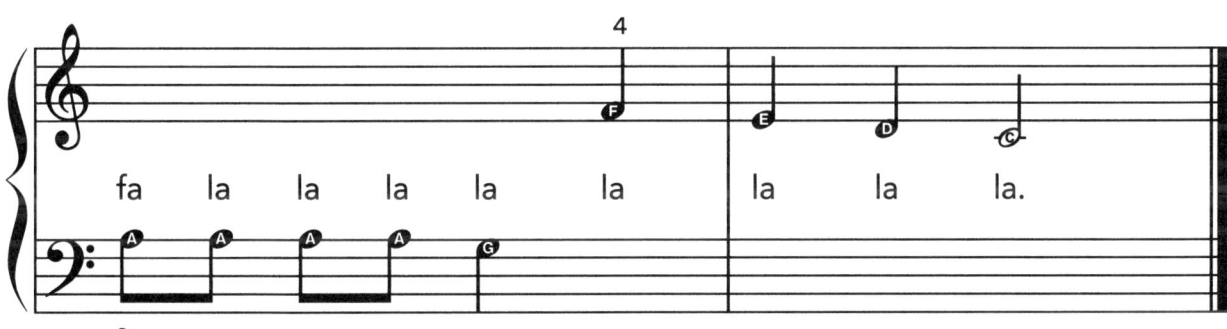

fa   la   la   la   la   la   la   la   la.

Jingle Bells

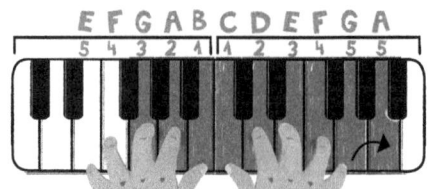

In this song, you'll need to stretch your right pinkie out to play A!

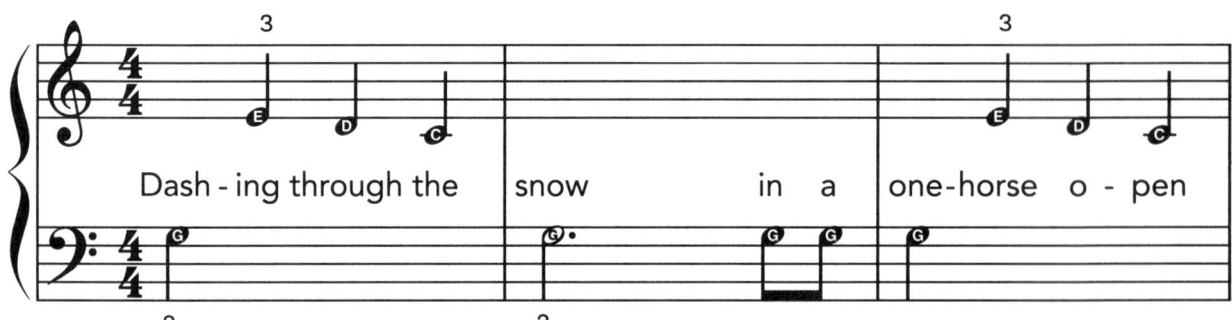

Dash - ing through the snow in a one-horse o - pen

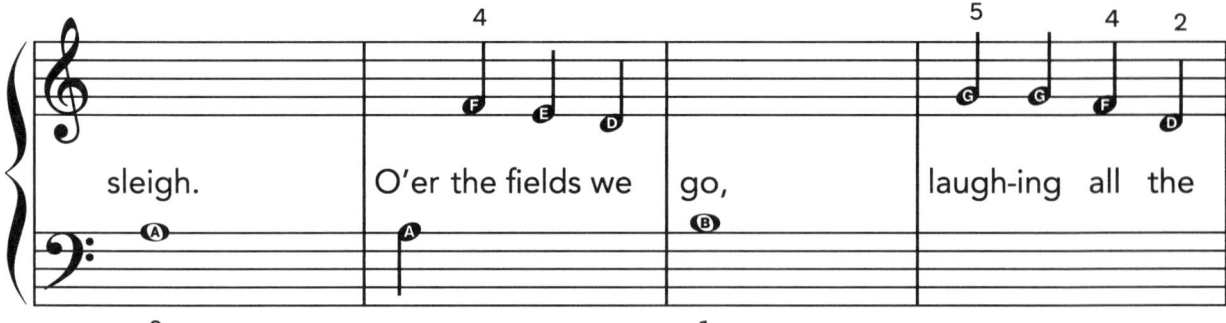

sleigh. O'er the fields we go, laugh-ing all the

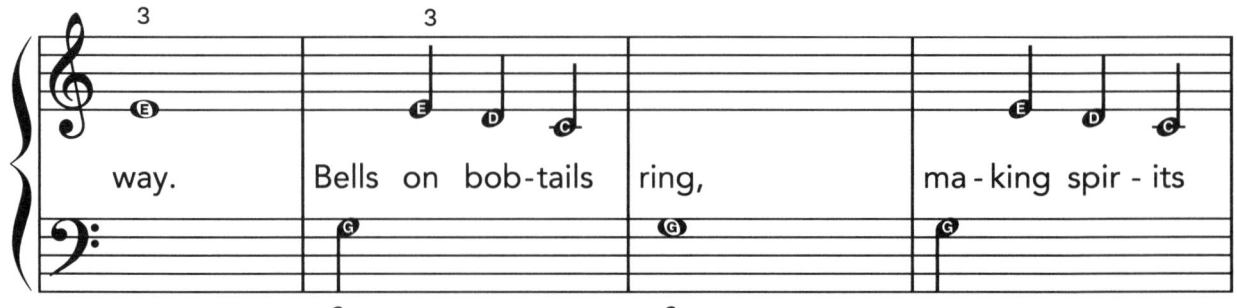

way. Bells on bob-tails ring, ma - king spir - its

The Twelve Days of Christmas

E F G A B C D E F G
5 4 3 2 1 1 2 3 4 5
F#

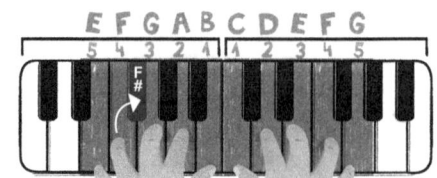

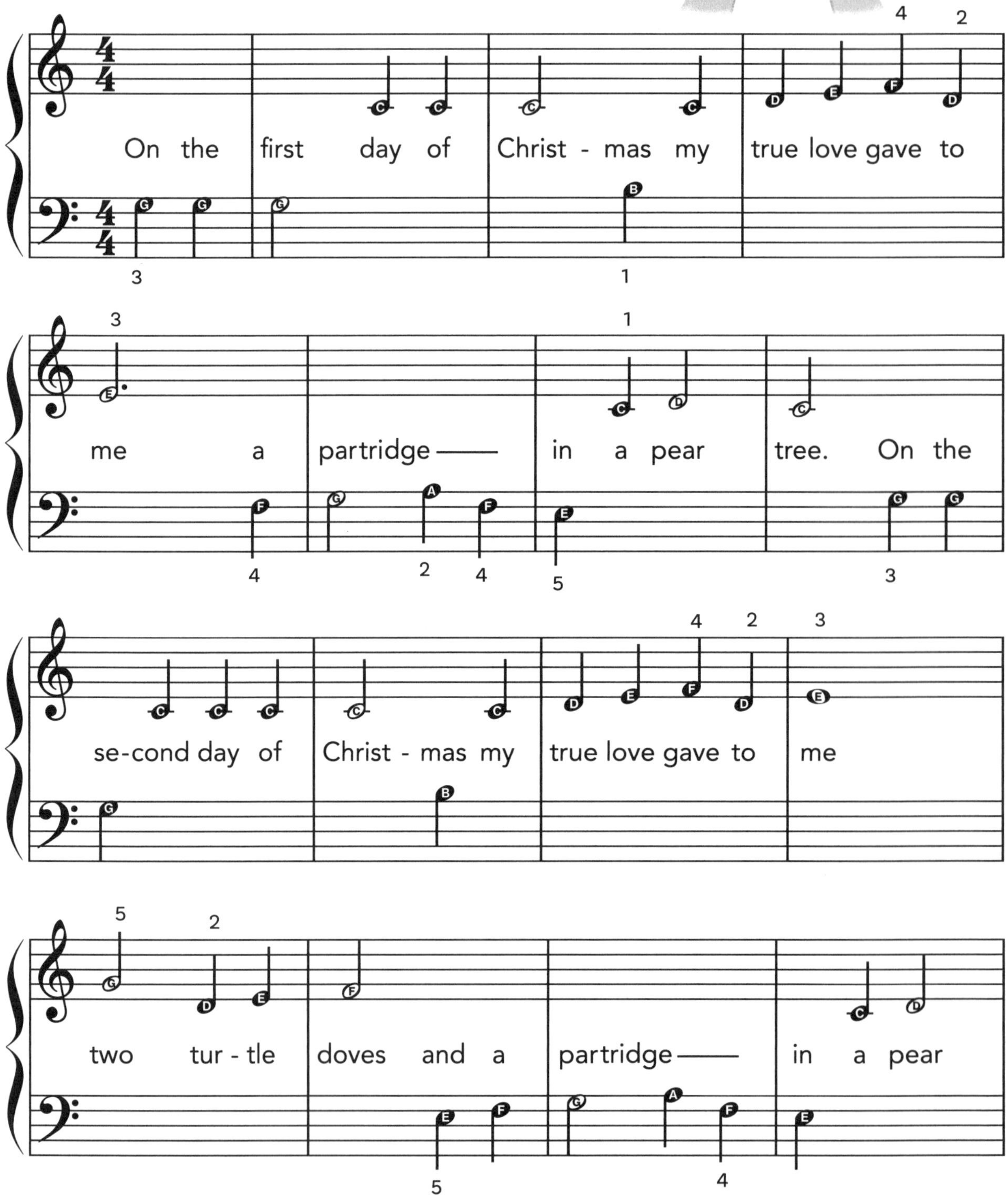

On the first day of Christ - mas my true love gave to
me a partridge —— in a pear tree. On the
se-cond day of Christ - mas my true love gave to me
two tur - tle doves and a partridge —— in a pear

Play 2 times!

continued

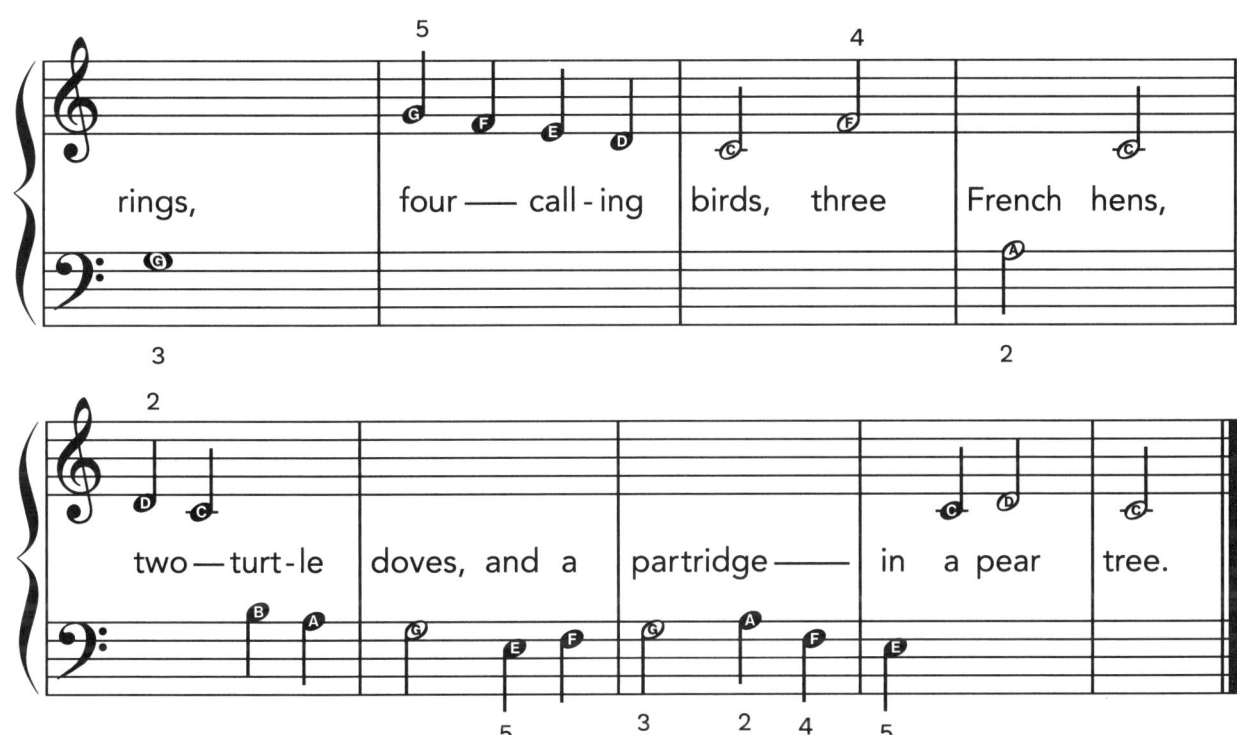

FUN FACT

To buy all the gifts in the song "The Twelve Days of Christmas" it would cost over $49,000 in today's money. Wow!

God Rest Ye Merry Gentlemen

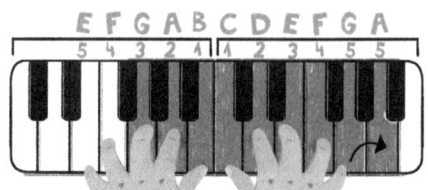

In this song, you'll need to stretch your right pinkie out to play A!

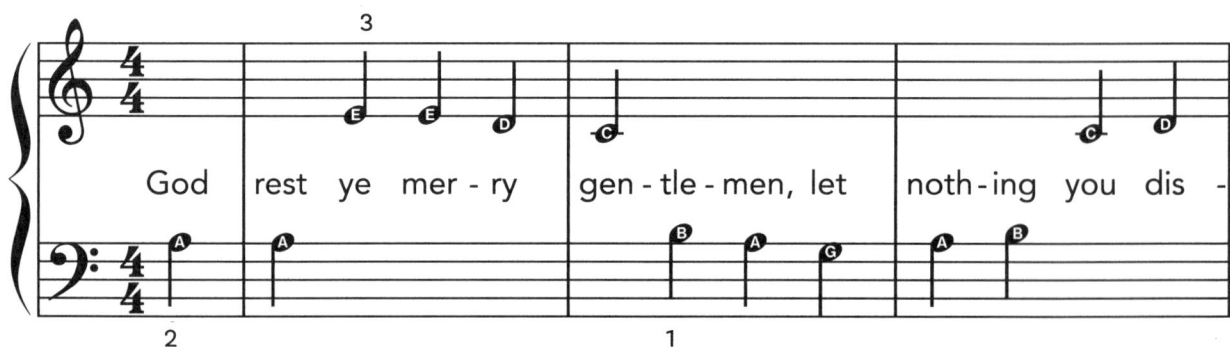

God | rest ye mer - ry | gen - tle - men, let | noth-ing you dis -

may. | Re - mem-ber Christ our | Sa - vior was | born on Christ-mas

Stretch your pinkie to play A

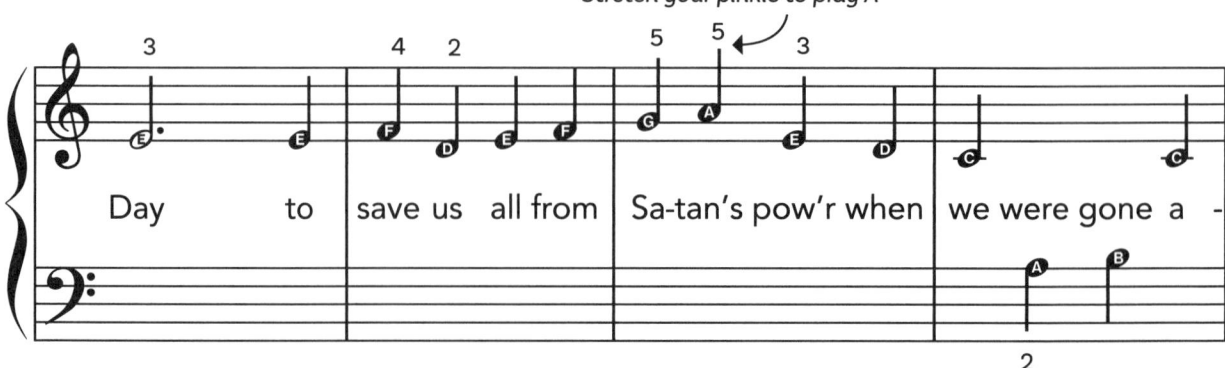

Day | to save us all from | Sa-tan's pow'r when | we were gone a -

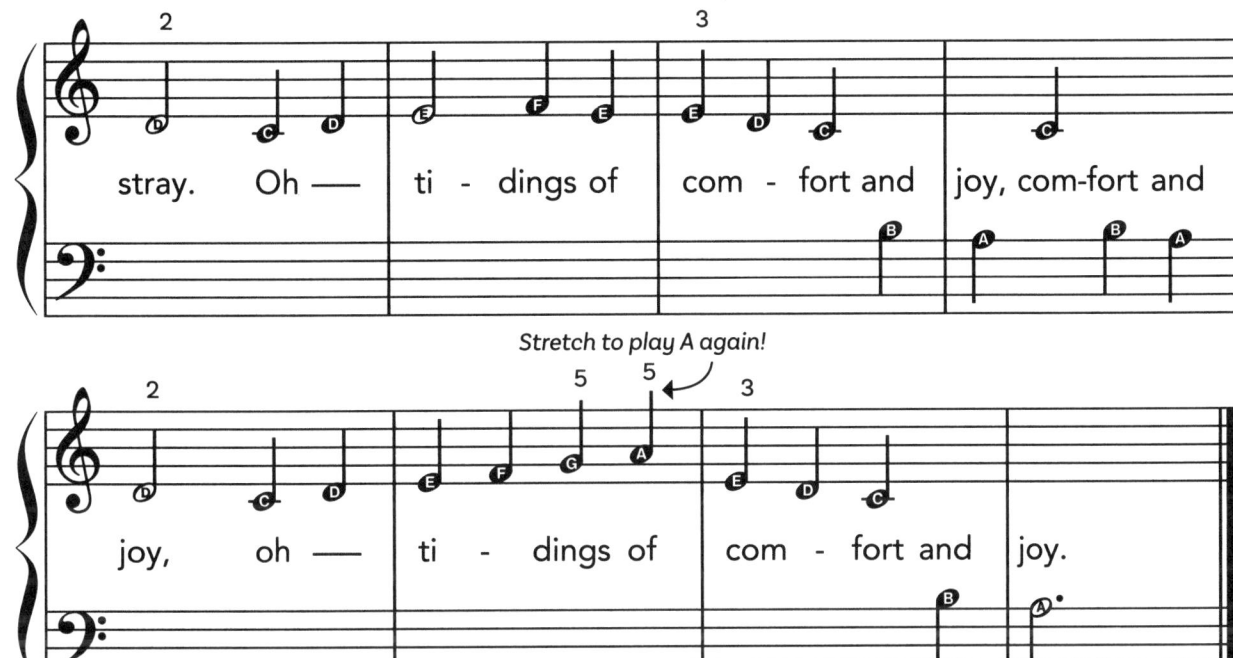

Stretch to play A again!

Joy to the World

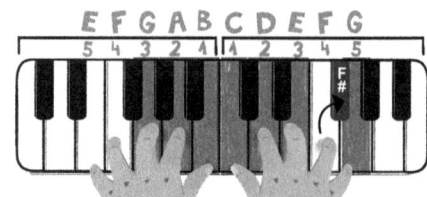

Every time you see a F#, stretch your 4th finger up to the sharp key!

Joy   to   the   world,   the   Lord   is   come.   Let

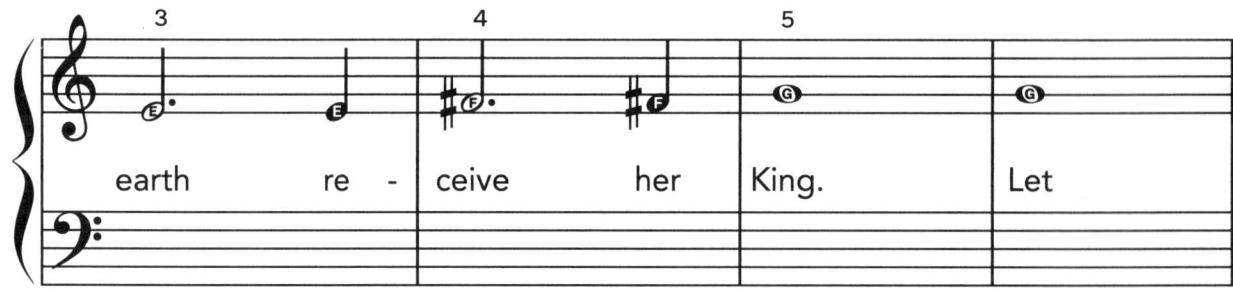

earth   re - ceive   her   King.   Let

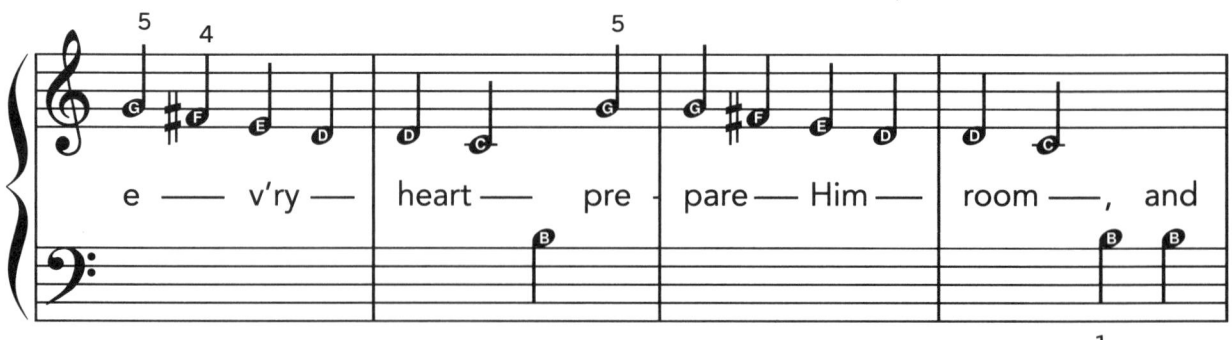

e —— v'ry ——   heart ——   pre - pare —— Him ——   room ——, and

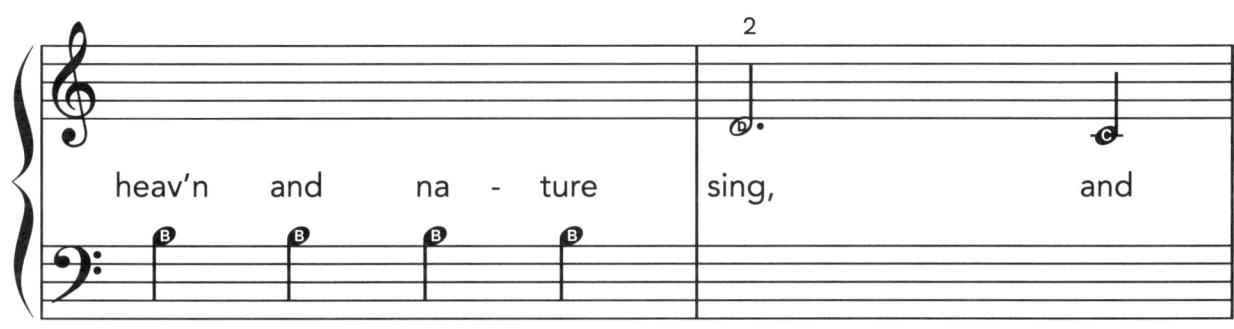

heav'n and na - ture sing, and

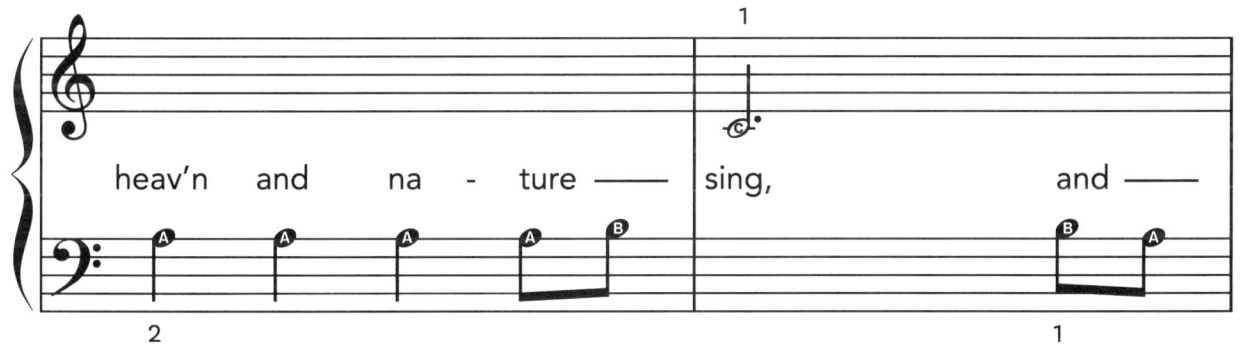

heav'n and na - ture —— sing, and ——

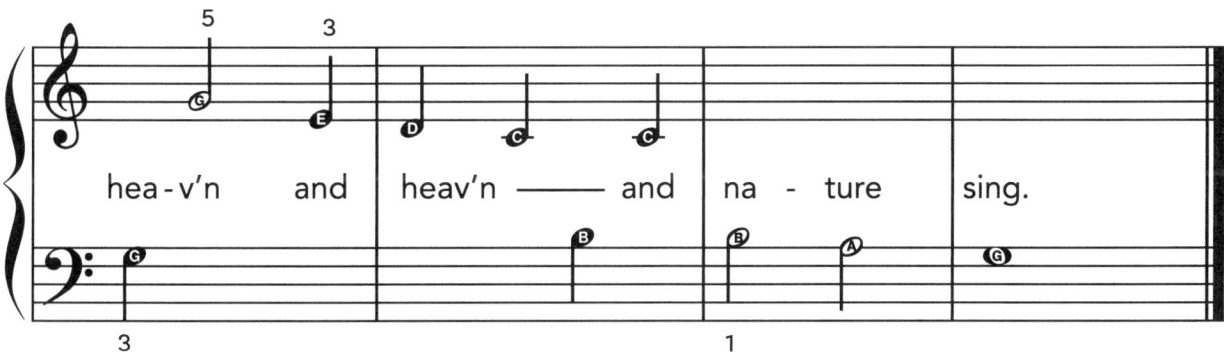

hea-v'n and heav'n —— and na - ture sing.

Auld Lang Syne

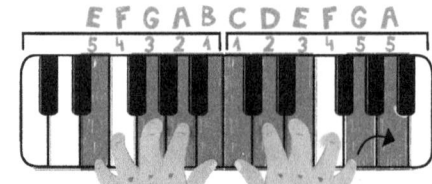

You'll need to reach your right pinkie out to play A several times in this song!

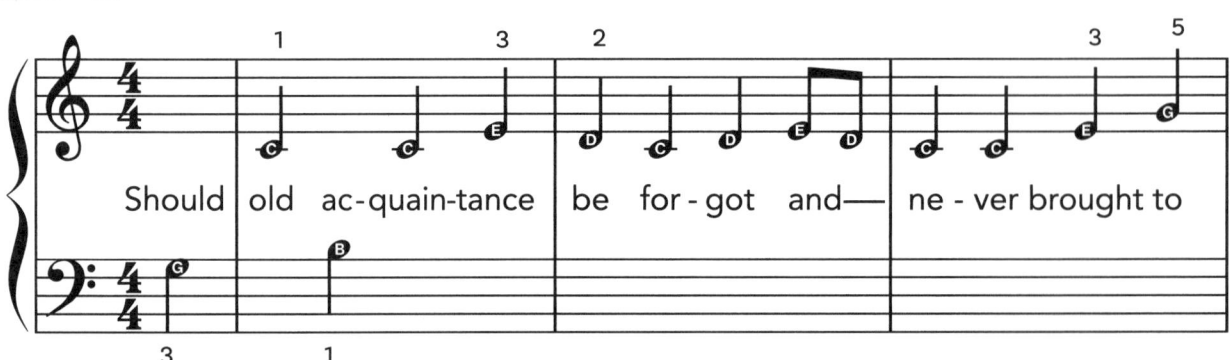

Should | old ac-quain-tance | be for-got and— | ne-ver brought to

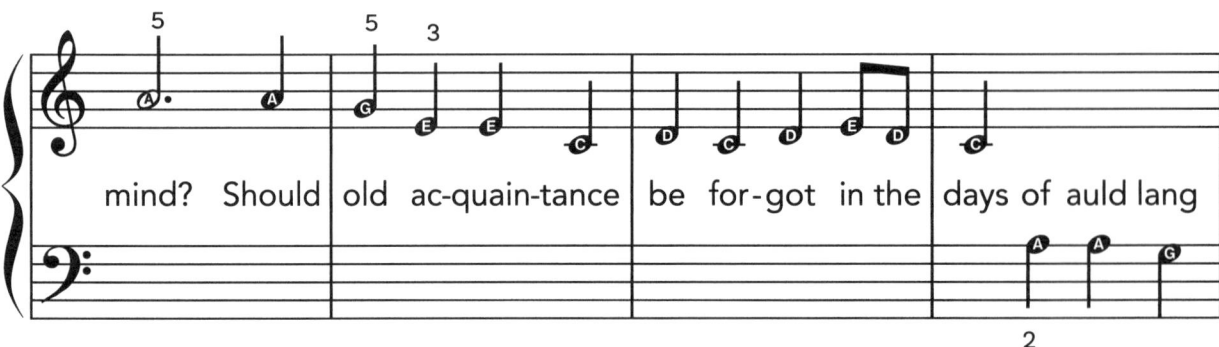

mind? Should | old ac-quain-tance | be for-got in the | days of auld lang

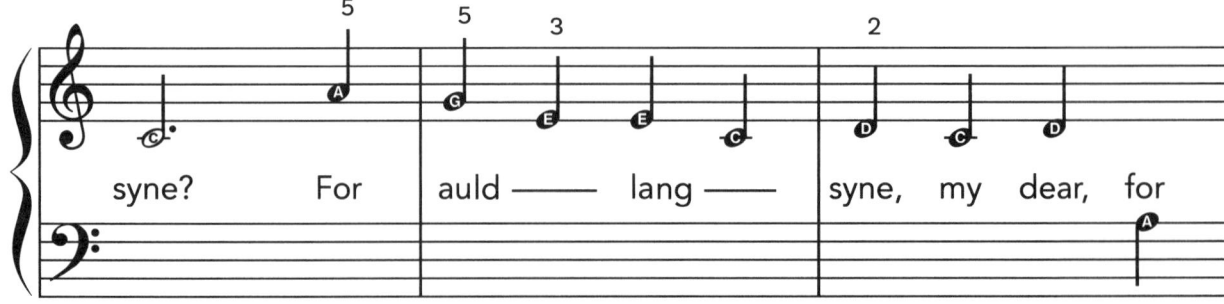

syne? For | auld —— lang —— | syne, my dear, for

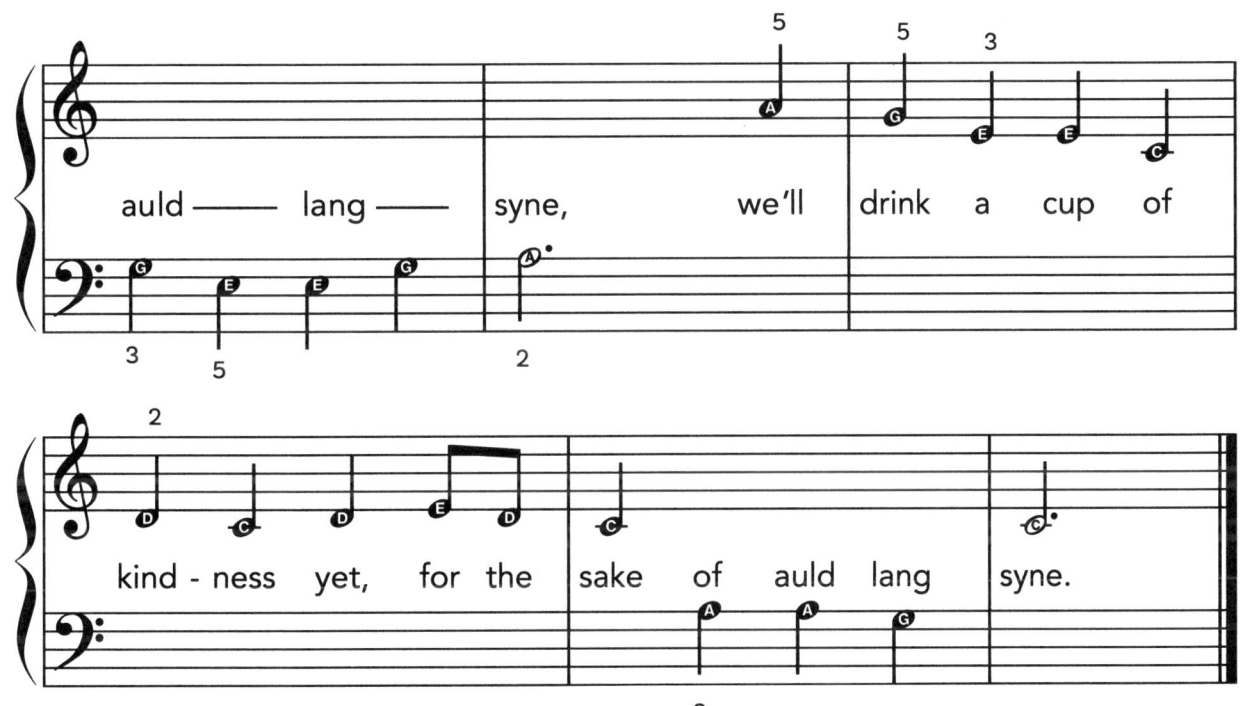

About the Author

Emily Norris, affectionately known as Ms. Emily, has been sharing her passion for music with students of all ages for over 15 years. As the founder of EBN Music, a small but vibrant music studio she established in 2020, Emily teaches piano and voice lessons tailored to each student, inspiring a lifelong love of music in all who walk through her door. Her dedication to her craft and her community earned her recognition in *Shoutout DFW*, a publication celebrating local entrepreneurs in the Dallas/Fort Worth area.

Emily holds a BA in music education from Freed-Hardeman University and an MSEd in educational technology from Missouri State University. She studied piano and voice under the direction of amazing teachers and mentors. She even excelled in trumpet, earning awards and accolades for her performances.

When she's not teaching, Emily cherishes time with her husband of 15 years, their beautiful daughter, born in 2024, and their two playful German shepherds. Whether she's helping students master their first Christmas carol or enjoying family time, Emily's love for music and teaching shines through in everything she does.

Parents, you can find Emily online on YouTube (youtube.com/@ebnmusic), Facebook (facebook.com/ebnmusic), Instagram (@ebn.music), and TikTok (@ebnmusic).

About the Illustrator

Malgorzata Detner is a Poland-based illustrator, born in 1989. She currently lives with her family in Warsaw. Her love of drawing began at a young age, influenced by her mother's paintings, but grew seriously when she decided to pursue art in middle school. Although Malgorzata initially pursued a career in costume design with an interest in Victorian dresses, her daughter's birth made her return to traditional painting and digital illustration. Influenced by old animation, mysterious, fantastic worlds, animals, and creatures in vibrant colors are what she likes drawing the most. She draws digitally but also likes to incorporate hand-painted textures into her work. Malgorzata loves creating illustrations that remind her of childhood memories.

Parents, you can find Malgorzata on Instagram (@mdetner.illustration) or at malgorzatadetner.com.

To my beautiful daughter, Molly.
May your soft giggles and
expressive coos blossom into
melodies as bright and
beautiful as you are.

Z Kids
An imprint of Zeitgeist™
A division of Penguin Random House LLC
1745 Broadway, New York, NY 10019
zeitgeistpublishing.com
penguinrandomhouse.com

ISBN: 9780593886045
Ebook ISBN: 9780593886038

Printed in the United States of America
2nd Printing

Illustrations by Malgorzata Detner
Book design by Erin Yeung
Author photograph © by Haylee Beth Photography
Illustrator photograph © 2022 by MDetner
Edited by Ada Fung

The authorized representative in the EU for product safety
and compliance is Penguin Random House Ireland, Morrison
Chambers, 32 Nassau Street, Dublin D02 YH68, Ireland.
https://eu-contact.penguin.ie

JOIN G-SHARP THE GIRAFFE FOR MORE PIANO FUN!

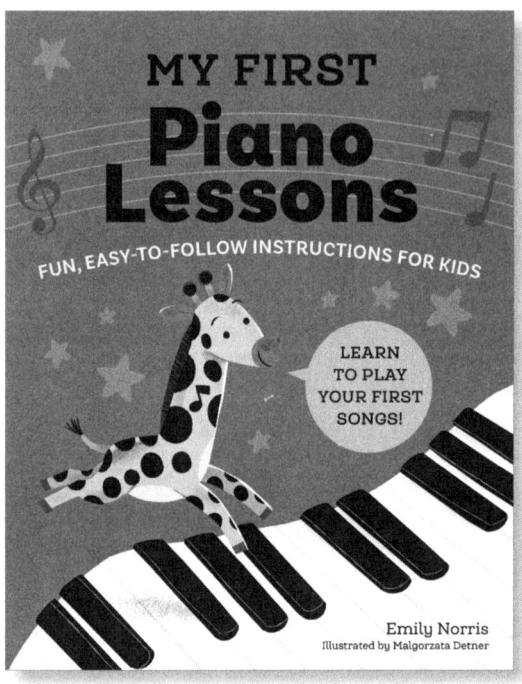

This beginner-friendly book of piano lessons is the perfect tool to unlock and nurture your child's love for the piano.

This songbook has 40 easy-to-learn tunes, clear music notation, and helpful hand positions for every song.

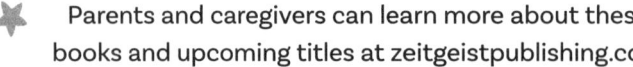